KNOW HIS WAY!

Cling to Christ for the Ride of Your Life!

JERI R. DANIEL

KNOW HIS WAY! by Jeri R. Daniel

ISBN 978-1-59755-271-4

Published by: ADVANTAGE BOOKS™
www.advbookstore.com

Library of Congress Control Number: 2011941630

Cover design by Pat Theriault

First Printing: December 2011
11 12 13 14 15 16 17 10 9 8 7 6 5 4 3 2 1
Printed in the United States of America

DEDICATION

This book is dedicated to Jesus Christ and all who have been with me on the ride of my life!

ENDORSEMENTS

Many times it seems that the very things we say "No Way!" to are the very things that God wants us to do! The real life stories in this book will capture your heart. The biblical references will strengthen your soul. The connectivity between stories will keep you hooked. The relevant subjects addressed will help to equip. Be ready to be encouraged to walk in faith as you say "Yes Way!" to the "No Way!"

Nathan Wilder
Minister of Students and Sports Outreach
First Baptist Church, Oviedo, Florida

Jeri Daniel writes with such simplicity and clarity as she shares her journey of faith through real life stories. As you read her book you will discover that our God can be trusted with the everyday situations that we all are involved in as we travel through life. I highly recommend ***KNOW HIS WAY!*** in the hope that each of us will see God working in our lives daily.

Reverend Herbert T. Long
Assistant Pastor
First Baptist Church, Oviedo, Florida

A very insightful book of personal stories from a lady committed to Christ and her family...enjoy!

Dr. Dwayne Mercer
Senior Pastor
First Baptist Church, Oviedo, Florida

Jeri has carefully chronicled significant "God moments" in her life that will serve as a powerful reminder of the providence of God in our own lives. It is critical that we all recognize God's past faithfulness so that our faith might be strengthened in future storms. Jeri's book is like a modern day Ebenezer stone that Samuel established to remind the children of Israel that the Lord had helped them in the past and that He would indeed help them in the future (I Samuel 7:12). As you read this excellent recollection of real life stories may you be stimulated to recall God's past work in your own life!

Chris Johnson
Senior Pastor
Grace Chapel Lancaster, California

ACKNOWLEDGMENTS

Ron, Amy, Lisa, Kara, Angie, Lydia, and Kaleb Daniel, I love my life with you! Next to Christ, you are definitely my greatest gifts!

To my church family, First Baptist Church of Oviedo, thank you for your continued prayers, support, and encouragement.

Pastor Mercer, Brother Herb, Nathan Wilder, and Chris Johnson your endorsement of the book is priceless to me.

Thank you to Melba and Dave Daniel for being such an active part of our family mission: POWER LOCK Worldwide *(Powerful Offering With Every Resource to make the Love Of Christ Known Worldwide).*

Bebe Seabolt (Mom, Nana), thank you yet again for "proof-listening" to everything and standing by my side. I love you!

Julie Cashion, thank you for your prayerful presence in this ministry. It means more than you know.

Mary Odell, Carol Daniel, Jill Moen, and Don (Dad) and Cory Freeman, I greatly appreciate your feedback.

Mike and Karen Janiczek and Pat Therriault, thank you for making it possible!

To everyone who played a part in any of our ***KNOW HIS WAY!*** stories, Thank you! You will recognize the one(s) about you! I am forever grateful to each and every one who encouraged me to know His way!

Table of Contents

Dedication 3

Endorsements 5

Acknowledgments 7

Preface: Buckle Up! 11

From Suicide to Salvation 13

Spouse Seeking, the Skateboard, and the Love of my Life 19

Painful Scars and Proper Healing (Pick that Scab and Heal!) 29

The Only Marriage Tool You'll Ever Need: The Screwdriver 37

Don't You Dare Write About Me In Your Prayer Journal! 43

Tithing, Tide, & Toilet Paper 49

Marshmallows, Pecan Pie, and the Trucks 55

Only for a Year (or Six) 63

Why Did I Mail That? I Can't Get it Back! 69

I Don't Know Her, but I'm Praying 75

Delivery from a Deadly Dime 81

Two Years: Five Moves, Three Jobs, and a Baby 89

Penny-Pinching and Provisions 97

Instruments of God 107

I Really *Was* Blind, But Now I See 117

Fertility May be Futile 125

In Awe of God 135
Extreme Home Makeover 141
The Baby Fix 153
Savor the Savior and ***KNOW HIS WAY!*** 159
Afterword: The Happiest Ending Ever! 169
Appendix: Tips for a Safe Ride 177

PREFACE

Buckle Up!

*K**NO**W HIS* ***WAY!*** is a collection of our family's favorite, incredible "coincidences," which point to God's presence, provision, and protection. Each one was documented throughout the years in my daily prayer journals. These are the stories that prompt the expressive, "NO WAY!" response, yet they undeniably reveal God's tender and powerful way. What a variety of creative means God uses to draw us to Him!

Many relevant topics are addressed, including: relationships, finances, fertility, healing, family, and ministry, just to list a few. Every written memory adds evidence to the rewards of prayer journaling. From spouse seeking to life saving, the reader will experience the roller coaster ride of faith that comes from "clinging to Christ." Inspiring each one to remember, record, and retell his or her own God stories, *K**NO**W HIS* ***WAY!*** magnifies glimpses of God's faithful characteristics.

Each chapter is not just "based on a true story," each chapter *is* a true story. Specific names and certain details have been intentionally left out in order to maintain the simplicity of the similar pattern from, "There's *no way!"* to "His way" to "No way!" Certainly, this book is not all inclusive. There are many more of our life chapters, which are not contained within the following pages. If your life has crossed with ours, perhaps one of those stories is in *your* book.

While some of the events cover the span of several years, others occurred in only a day or two. In the midst of a trial, time sometimes seems to stand still; however, when looking back after the "ending" has taken place, the stories of our lives take on a simple, "Before," "During," and "After" outline. Of course there are some stories in our lives that will remain unfinished until our life here on earth is over. What an exciting and glorious ending that will be for all who have accepted God's free gift through Jesus! If you are unsure about your own "ending," please read this book's ending, which will explain how you *can* be sure.

It is my prayer that multitudes will come to know Christ and the depth of His love through my life and my family. We are not "above" anyone else, by any means. We just want to serve the God, because He *is* above all. It is my desire for every person to grow in an affectionate, personal relationship with Jesus Christ in daily, two-way communication with Him. By reading the Bible—God's Word to us—and praying to Him, by speaking or writing, we can more easily recognize His presence every day. How comforting life is as we learn to *K**NO**W HIS **WAY!***

From Suicide to Salvation

Topics covered: *Suicide, where will I go when I die, God's love and forgiveness, salvation, hope, and peace.*

For as long as I can remember, I dreamed of living "happily ever after." I sought approval from others, hoping to feel satisfied through their acceptance, and, while I was temporarily fulfilled by words of affirmation, a rejection of any kind drained me. I became a chameleon: In my quest to feel love, I would become what another person thought I should be. I longed to be loved like a fairy tale princess.

After being rejected one too many times, I planned my suicide. I was an emotional mess, so self-consumed by my own feelings of disappointment and dissatisfaction. I simply didn't want to feel pain, anger, or sadness ever again. There was only one problem keeping me from following through: What would happen to me after I died? Would I go to heaven or hell? Would I just not exist anymore? I had been raised to believe that Jesus is God and to celebrate Christmas and Easter by going to church. I had just enough information to be absolutely *unsure* of where I would go if I acted on my suicidal thoughts. In sobs, I cried out to God to show me for sure if He was real and how I could be sure about heaven. I postponed my plans until I could find the answer.

The following week, our public high school had an assembly with a guest speaker. The topic? Suicide! The speaker actually played a cassette of a boy saying good-bye to his mother just before the bang of the gunshot echoed throughout the gym. Hundreds of kids did not make a sound. Being a public school, the speaker could not say much spiritually, but he invited all of us to come to a local church that same evening where we could hear more.

He was a very entertaining speaker, but I was shocked at how many familiar faces showed up that night. At the end of the event, we were asked to close our eyes and raise our hands if we wanted to be sure where we would go when we died. Once our hands were up, he had us come down to the front of the church to meet one on one with counselors who were waiting to talk to us individually. I asked my questions and prayed the prayer to ensure that I would go to heaven one day, but I left there with only part of the truth. I understood that I could go to heaven by believing that Jesus, God's Son, had died and that he was resurrected three days later. What I did not understand was that I did not need to earn my way to heaven, because Jesus had already paid for everything in full.

For three years I struggled to be good enough to "hold my place" in heaven. These were the most sin-filled years of my life. I was like a yo-yo. I failed, and then I promised to do better, and then failed again. I really wanted to please God, but I still wanted so badly to have the acceptance of others. These desires were continually conflicting. As a parent sometimes allows a child to suffer logical consequences, I also suffered from the effects of my poor choices.

Then, one day, I finally understood what Jesus had done for me. It was as though I had been struggling in the quick sand of life, sinking deeper and deeper as I tried to save myself. Once I acknowledged my own inability, asked for forgiveness, and realized the depth of God's love for me, I gave up every area of myself to Christ. He freed me from the pulls of sin, washed me clean, and gave me new life. My "happily ever after" had just begun! I am truly a princess, the adopted child of the King of Kings!

From Suicide to Salvation

Cling to Christ for the Ride of Your Life!

There's No Way!

If you were to die today, where would you go?

If God asked you why He should let you into heaven, what would you say?

Know His Way!

> ***In the same way your Father in heaven is not willing that any of these little ones should perish.*** Matthew 18:14
>
> ***For God so loved the world that he gave his one and only Son, that whoever believes in him shall not perish but have eternal life.*** John 3:16
>
> ***The Lord is not slow in keeping his promise, as some understand slowness. Instead he is patient with you, not wanting anyone to perish, but everyone to come to repentance.*** 2 Peter 3:9

From Suicide to Salvation

Write your own *KNOW HIS WAY!*

No Way!
Briefly write your own salvation story with the simple pattern below:

Before (There's no way!):

During (Know His way!):

After (No way!):

Spouse Seeking, the Skateboard, and the Love of my Life

Topics covered: *Purity, God's timing, spouse seeking, and salvation*

With the dream that I would one day get married and have a house full of children, I believed it was all up to me to find my future husband. I began the search at an early age. Quite honestly, I remember at the ripe old age of six, wondering if the cute boy I played with on the playground may be "the one." I was never "not allowed" to have a boyfriend, so I felt I should search for "the one" in order to not miss him when our paths happened to cross. What was innocent and cute as a little girl, was hurtful and confusing as a teen. I truly believed this was my purpose in life. I wanted to learn to cook and keep house, to take care of babies and children, and I wanted to be the wife that a husband would want to spend time with. I learned to take an interest in cars, carpentry, and the sports that I could figure out, but these were not necessarily my own interests. They were for the purpose of preparing to be the wife that a husband would love…and not leave.

After my emotionally painful brush with suicide and my "fire insurance" prayer, I graduated high school and began college. If I was to be married in my early twenties, as I had planned, I would have to hurry to find my husband! I knew that I wanted to be right with God; so, I attended church more than I ever had before. During the week, I sought the popularity of people, and on Sundays I sought God's forgiveness. I was tormented. In the midst of each relationship, my fear of rejection increasingly clouded my every thought until I had chased away yet another boy. My active search for love repeatedly resulted in loneliness. Ultimately, self disgust ended my search shortly after a date rape, which I pretended did not happen. I was sorely alone. I told no one. I promised God to do better. I would save myself for my wedding day.

A few months later, my brother-in-law begged me to meet a guy at his church. Apparently, the young man went to another church, but would be visiting his parents that coming Sunday. I told my brother-in-law that I was done with dating! If God wanted me to marry someone, He would have to just put him in my path without me looking! Since I had been visiting their church regularly anyway, I finally agreed to meet the guy, but not as a blind date--and the guy was *not* to know that it was a potential set up.

That Sunday during the service, my sister quietly pointed out an elderly gentleman on the other side of the congregation, who sat in front of the guy she wanted me to see. She laughed hysterically at my reaction, and then told me to look in the row behind that man. When I leaned forward to see, I instantly saw a young man leaning forward to see me! *He knew!* I was mad, but he was so handsome that I was glad to get to meet him.

We hit it off immediately. Ironically, he had recently told his parents that he was done with dating and had accepted that he was probably never going to marry. He had been coerced to meet me, too. With similar discouragements, we both now had high moral standards and a detailed mental "shopping list." We wasted no time in beginning what was more like a series of interviews than dates. Could this really be the one? I hoped so.

After our first date, I was often invited to Sunday dinner at his parents' house after church. The first time, I was a nervous wreck. What if his family did not accept me? With butterflies in my stomach, I was warmly welcomed, and I felt at home with these people. I remember knocking over his dad's ice tea, and he handled it so graciously. At one of these meals, I noticed a certain way that his dad seemed to be looking at me.

He then asked me, "Do you, by any chance, ride a skateboard?" *Oh, no!* I suddenly knew why he had been looking at me that way. We both remembered.

"Yes, I do," I answered sheepishly.

He then addressed his family, "Do you all remember a few months back when I told you about the blonde girl riding her skateboard near the UCF library?" They did.

"Was that you?" he asked me.

"Yes, it was."

His version of the story: On a Saturday, as he approached the sloped path that led to the entrance of the library, a cute, young, blonde girl came sailing down the hill on a skateboard toward the street. As she flew down toward the grass, in one fell swoop she flipped the skateboard up, caught it in her arms, and kept running, never missing a step. He was impressed!

My version of the story: On a Saturday, a previous boyfriend had been teaching me how to ride my skateboard on campus, since it was empty of people then. Two drives sloped down from the library entrance. He went down one, and I went down the other, so I was alone. While I had learned quite a bit, I was terrible at stopping when riding fast.

My routine was to ride down the slope crossing the sidewalk and to run into the grass on the other side, at which point I would hop off and sprint out the rest of the momentum. This worked fine for me, except for one time; as I flew down the hill, I saw the impending doom of a collision with a gentleman. I could not stop! Zooming into the grass, I hopped off the skateboard. Afraid that the board, itself, would collide with him, I kicked down on the back of it as I jumped off, hoping to prevent it from crashing into him. Instead, the board flipped up toward me; so, I grabbed it and had to keep jogging in order to not fall. That gentleman was now sitting at the dinner table retelling the story of my "slick trick."

With the complete approval and blessing of both families, Ron and I were engaged five months after we met.

Read this excerpt from my book, Savor the Savior (Pen, Bible, Ice Cream!):

> I finally found a Christian man. He actually accepted me, even after I revealed to him every past failure I could remotely recall. He was willing to walk with me together toward God, and we were to be married the following year.
>
> One Sunday morning, I finally found the missing link. I sat with my future husband and with my pastor as I prepared to be baptized by immersion. I had already been baptized by sprinkling at a previous church, but I knew I had not been right with God at that time. To me, *this* baptism was supposed to be a symbol of my promise to God that I would try *even harder* to live as I knew He wanted me to. Besides, I needed to be baptized by immersion in order to join my fiancée's church, where we were planning to be married in only a few months.
>
> During the traditional conversation which was routine before the baptism, the pastor asked me the age old question, "If you were to stand at the gates of Heaven today, and were asked why you should be allowed in, what would you say?" Well… hmmm… I hadn't ever thought of it like that before… well… hmmm…??? Because… well… hmmm… because…I have *really tried* to be good." *"God, You know how hard I've been trying,*

don't You? That counts, right?" As I glanced up and saw the eyes of my poor fiancée turn to saucers, I pretty much guessed that I had gotten *that* answer wrong. The pastor cleared his throat and all but elbowed my hubby-to-be in the ribs so he would catch his jaw from hitting the floor. Would I lose him now?

As I listened to the pastor's explanation, I suddenly realized that I had been struggling so hard to do something that had already been done for me long ago. Christ had already paid the price of *all* my sins. It was finished. What a relief! I was so thankful to know that I was not responsible for earning my way to Heaven! My response that day was with absolute understanding, deepest gratitude, and a peaceable relief. My motivation for baptism was no longer distorted. To be baptized was a picture of all of those sins (that quick sand) being washed away from me. I was now free to walk with my Lord and serve Him in response to my utmost appreciation. I was just beginning to understand how much I was adored by the One who made me. He valued me enough to give His only Son in my place so that I could live with Him forever. My search for love was finally over. Jesus Christ *had* to be my One *True* Love!

In response to this amazing love shown to me, I dedicated my life to the Lord. I was eager to find out as much as I could about this new Love of my life.

Spouse Seeking, the Skateboard, and the Love of my Life

Cling to Christ for the Ride of Your Life!

There's No Way!
What can you do to show God that you trust Him with your spouse (past, present, or future)?

Know His Way!

> ***For I know the plans I have for you," declares the LORD, "plans to prosper you and not to harm you, plans to give you hope and a future.*** Jeremiah 29:11
>
> ***How can a young person stay on the path of purity? By living according to your word. I seek you with all my heart; do not let me stray from your commands.*** Psalm 119:9, 10
>
> ***But if they cannot control themselves, they should marry, for it is better to marry than to burn with passion.***
> 1 Corinthians 7:9

Spouse Seeking, the Skateboard, and the Love of my Life

Write your own *KNOW HIS WAY!*

No Way!
Briefly write your own spouse seeking story with the simple pattern below. If your story is unfinished, leave those portions blank:

Before (There's no way!):

During (Know His way!):

After (No way!):

Painful Scars and Proper Healing (Pick that Scab and Heal!)

Topics covered: *Relationship healing, mother-daughter relationship, counseling, Biblical reconciliation, forgiveness, and self-evaluation*

Baggage. Oh, how much emotional baggage I brought into my marriage! Less than two months after our wedding day, my husband and I sought assistance from our pastor. Surely, someone could help us to better adjust to the frustrations we were both dealing with. After our first session, the pastor told us that he wanted to meet with me separately in order to work through my past. Knowing the severity of my own mood swings, and the pulls of depression, I gladly agreed.

This was the first time I had ever met with a counselor by myself, but I was relieved to have help. I truly wanted to get better. He began by telling me that it sounded like I had some anger toward my parents. *That was an understatement!* He encouraged me to talk about the effects of my parents' divorce, as well as my current relationship with each one of them.

My dad had traveled a great deal when I was growing up. I always wanted to be closer to him. My mom had often had to deal with my teenage rebellion alone when he was traveling, so our relationship was extremely stormy. Along with my sisters, I also felt responsible for her, once we had all moved away and she was alone. On several occasions, I was torn between pleasing my mom and pleasing my husband.

I left the church with homework to complete before the following week. I was to write an in depth letter to each of my parents telling every past anger or hurt that I had ever had. These would not be delivered, but would be read to the counselor the next time we met. When I returned and read aloud each letter, I realized that it was the first I had ever let all of those feelings out. He soon gave me my next assignment. I was told to interview my dad in order to begin a new and growing relationship. This would be easy and should be enjoyable.

My relief soon turned to dread, though, as I received the rest of the assignment. In order to restore my relationship with my mom, that pastor told me to set up a meeting with her in order to read the letter I had written. *What?!* She would be crushed! She had already been through so much; I could not be the one to "push her over the edge." Couldn't I interview her, too?

He then asked me if I would rather risk losing my relationship with my mother or my husband. If I chose not to address the issues with my mom, he assured me that my marriage would never be what it could be. If I did follow through with my mom, I risked isolation and rejection from her and my three sisters; however, we may just end up with a properly healed, thriving relationship based on open honesty and truth. Begrudgingly, I agreed.

The interview with my dad went without a hitch. I realized that I had never heard him tell his own childhood story before. It opened my eyes to see him in a whole new light, and I was anxious to get to know him even more. I enjoyed spending time with him, and I was especially intrigued with the mysteries about him which unraveled through his story-telling.

Since my mom was always an advocate of counseling, she readily agreed to meet with me in order to help me complete my homework assignment. Neither of us knew quite what to expect. After some nervous chit-chat, I told her I was supposed to read my letter to her. As I poured it all out, I tried not to look her in the eyes, knowing the depths of hurt I would find in them. For her, I suppose it was like trying to take a sip of water from a fire hose. It was messy and painful. We spent hours into the night in tears, as we mutually fought to repair our past together. At the end of the night, we were both exhausted.

For the next three weeks, I was unofficially exiled from the family. No one wanted to talk to me. All of them were mad at me for the hurt I had "unnecessarily" caused. As my mom sought to make sense of it all, she asked questions of my sisters. Another sister opened up a bit with both my mom and with me, which was pivotal in the healing process.

My husband said that sometimes when a wound does not heal, the doctor has to do surgery to clean the infection out before it can heal properly. That is what God did on that day. Today, my mom and I are truly the best of friends. Because our relationship is based on complete truth—God's Truth—we have a bond that is beyond belief. Our relationship with each other only compliments my marriage. Her counsel is unbiased, based on God's Word through prayerful consideration. She is quick to seek forgiveness when she messes up, and she is a beautiful example for me to follow.

Painful Scars and Proper Healing (Pick that Scab and Heal!)

Cling to Christ for the Ride of Your Life!

There's No Way!

Is there a relationship in your life that needs proper healing through the Great Physician?

What actions do you plan to take?

Know His Way!

> ***"Why do you look at the speck of sawdust in your brother's eye and pay no attention to the plank in your own eye? How can you say to your brother, 'Let me take the speck out of your eye,' when all the time there is a plank in your own eye? You hypocrite, first take the plank out of your own eye, and then you will see clearly to remove the speck from your brother's eye.*** Matthew 7:3-5
>
> ***If your brother or sister sins, go and point out their fault, just between the two of you. If they listen to you, you have won them over.*** Matthew 18:15
>
> ***"Honor your father and mother"—which is the first commandment with a promise—"so that it may go well with you and that you may enjoy long life on the earth."*** Ephesians 6:2-3

The Only Marriage Tool You'll Ever Need: The Screwdriver

Topics covered: *Biblical marriage principles, submission, power of prayer, and relationships*

Some marriages start out with the first year of honeymoon bliss, but I have often jokingly said that our marriage did not really begin until after the first two and a half years. It took us that long to work out the initial kinks. Upon returning from our two week honeymoon, we moved in temporarily with Ron's parents for three weeks until our apartment was ready. During that time, we spontaneously bought two puppies: a golden retriever and a Yorkshire terrier.

We then rented a condo from my dad, which we shared with my sister. She had two Yorkshire terriers. My sister and I were still in college, and my husband worked a regular job until Hurricane Hugo hit South Carolina. He then left for six weeks to work as a roofer in order to build up our savings. We met in Georgia once for Thanksgiving, and then did not see each other again until he returned just in time for my graduation in mid-December. At that point, neither of us had a job. I searched for a teaching position, and Ron prepared to go back to college. We had at least ten stressors too many.

As a new follower of Christ, I read a chapter of my Bible each night before bed. It made more sense to me when I read it that way, and I was learning in leaps and bounds. Ron and I both got more involved in church, which we enjoyed together, but our marriage was still very rocky. We did not yet know how to "fight fair," and our expectations of each other were exceedingly high. This led to disappointment and anger. Don't get me wrong; we had a blast together in between the fights, but we were both often out of control emotionally. I had met my match!

One day in particular, as things flared out of control in a flash, I suddenly remembered to stop and pray. I did not pray out loud, but I did get on my knees by the couch with my eyes closed. Before long, Ron joined in next to me. It led to a calm conversation and a word picture that would save our marriage from crumbling.

Now, my husband, Ron, is an electrical engineer, and he is a teacher. He is definitely analytical, but he is also very much a people person. While we have obvious differences, we are also alike in many ways. We both are very social, and we especially love to laugh and play. We are easily touched by what children say and do. We also both are "fixers." For me, this applies to problems people have. For Ron, this applies to everything under the sun…unless he can figure out a way to fix that, too.

My hubby is also the very *best* at fixing just about everything. I can attest to this. He is a superhero minus the weird outfit. Since one man cannot possibly have time to fix everything, he constantly has a myriad of projects in the works; so when Ron came up with a word picture for me to better understand him, he used one that made perfect sense to both of us. It is simple, yet profound, and we have used it numerous times over the years.

Ron told me that he was like a screw going into drywall. God was already working on him as the Screwdriver, and His way would hold, but…I was like a hammer, and I was getting in the way of God. As a result, the screw was getting damaged and everything around was crumbling. God's way may take longer, but He is the perfect Tool, and His way will strongly endure. Let the hammer rest!

The Only Marriage Tool You'll Ever Need: The Screwdriver

Cling to Christ for the Ride of Your Life!

There's No Way!
When are you most tempted to be a hammer, and are you willing to let God be the Screwdriver?

Know His Way!

> ***Do two walk together unless they have agreed to do so?***
> Amos 3:3
>
> ***However, each one of you also must love his wife as he loves himself, and the wife must respect her husband.***
> Ephesians 5:33
>
> ***Love is patient, love is kind. It does not envy, it does not boast, it is not proud. It does not dishonor others, it is not self-seeking, it is not easily angered, it keeps no record of wrongs. Love does not delight in evil but rejoices with the truth. It always protects, always trusts, always hopes, always perseveres. Love never fails.*** 1 Corinthians 13:4-8a

TIP: Try first replacing the words for "love" in 1 Corinthians 13 with your own name. Next, replace those same words with "Jesus."

The Only Marriage Tool You'll Ever Need: The Screwdriver

Write your own *K**NO**W HIS **WAY!***

No Way!

Briefly write your own hammer/screwdriver story with the simple pattern below. If your story is unfinished, leave those portions blank:

Before (There's no way!):

During (Know His way!):

After (No way!):

Don't You Dare Write About Me in Your Prayer Journal!

Topics covered: *Journaling, power of prayer, praising God through story-telling, and testimonies*

In my first in-depth Bible study class, we were required to keep a journal of our prayers. I bought a small notebook and set it up according to the instructions. My written prayer requests were rather generic and bulletized. At this point in our marriage, we had moved into a tiny two-bedroom duplex—just the four of us—my husband, myself, and our two dogs. I now had a job teaching kindergarten, which I absolutely loved, and Ron was in his last year of college. We were dirt poor, but things were looking up!

While I loved my precious, four pound Yorkshire terrier lap dog, Ron equally adored his overly zealous, playful golden retriever, who truly thought he also was a lap dog. Both dogs brought us a great deal of joy and an even greater deal of work and expense. My little Yorkie had an incredibly annoying habit of piddling "somewhere" on the carpet or on the leg of the couch, but the piddle was too tiny to locate without crawling around on my belly, sniffing like a hound dog. Ron's sweet, but massive, retriever had a powerfully happy tail that smacked everything in sight, and our close quarters were simply too close for him. He rambunctiously chewed apart our couch and our carpet, and he bounded undisciplined through the hotel room sized apartment we called home. Something had to be done!

I, of course, chose to pray about the problem with Ron's dog first. It was a generic prayer, since I had no solutions in mind. I simply wrote, "Please take care of Casey." A few days later we boarded him with our vet while we went on vacation. Within a week of my written prayer, we were notified by the vet that Casey was found dead in his kennel. *He was only a year old!* They did an autopsy and found that he had a rare genetic condition, which caused him to die in his sleep. We were heart-broken. We returned to a much quieter, calmer home, but we sorely missed him.

About a month later, my Yorkshire terrier's piddling problem had progressed. He was literally out of control. I simply worded my prayer in my still new prayer journal, "Please take care of Joey." A week later, I gave Joey a bath outside and had not yet put his collar back on his damp fur. Suddenly, a parade of dogs bounded down the middle of the road after a hot Chow-Chow. Joey took off, full speed ahead. I sprinted after him, along with the other dog owners in the neighborhood. The whole pack disappeared into the thick woods nearby and lost the trailing humans. My husband drove his truck into the woods, but did not see them. Expecting the dogs to come out on the other side, he drove around, but the only dog that did not come out was ours. It was as though he just disappeared in the midst of the woods. We searched for hours, for days, for weeks, but we never did find our little dog. Our house now stayed clean, but I missed him dearly.

As sad as we were to lose both of our beloved pets, we could not deny the peace that came over our home as a result. Could it just be a coincidence that each dog "left" one week after my written prayers? I didn't think so. I believed that God had intervened. I had never witnessed anything like this before. The response we got from others when we shared our "weird" story was similar. In light of what happened to each dog, Ron's dad laughingly summed it up the best: "Don't you dare write about me in your prayer journal!"

Don't You Dare Write About Me in Your Prayer Journal!

Cling to Christ for the Ride of Your Life!

There's No Way!
What details from your daily life will you completely hand over to God?

If you do not already have a prayer journal, consider getting one today. *See my previous books for more journaling tips:* *Savor the Savior* *and* *Savor the Savior for Kids.*

Know His Way!

> ***And pray in the Spirit on all occasions with all kinds of prayers and requests.*** Ephesians 6:18a
>
> ***I call on you, my God, for you will answer me; turn your ear to me and hear my prayer.*** Psalm 17:6
>
> ***If you believe, you will receive whatever you ask for in prayer.*** Matthew 21:22

Don't You Dare Write About Me in Your Prayer Journal!

Write your own *KNOW HIS WAY!*

No Way!
Briefly write your own prayer journal story with the simple pattern below. If your story is unfinished, leave those portions blank:

Before (There's no way!):

During (Know His way!):

After (No way!):

Tithing, Tide, & Toilet Paper

Topics covered: *Stewardship, tithing, God's provision, obedience, faith, and prayer*

During my husband's last semester at college, we especially struggled financially. Around the time that tuition was due and books had to be purchased, our bank account bottomed out. One month in particular, it seemed that every bill was due at once, and we were in desperate need of a trip to the grocery store. Ron and I looked over the bills trying to decide which bill *not* to pay, but each one had looming consequences that we could not afford. We narrowed it down to either our tithe or our groceries.

By groceries, I mean everything! We purposely used the restroom while out in public in order to save the last of our toilet paper. Our laundry was on hold waiting for detergent. Our pantry was as bare as Old Mother Hubbard's. The only thing in it was a can of beans, which my sister had given me, because she didn't care for them. The choice seemed obvious, except for one thing: When we got married, we made a promise to God to trust Him and test Him by tithing—no matter what. We paid our tithe and prayed, not knowing how we would make it through the next two weeks before pay day.

The next day, Ron was killing time between classes at the small student center on campus. As he shot pool, he heard over the sound system the familiar UCF radio station. The DJ offered two free tickets to the first caller for that night's comedy show with a famous comedian. Ron used the pool hall phone and won! What a perfect free date night!

The comedian's specialty was word humor. The show began with a short film which featured humorous real signs from around the world. He then did a hilarious stand up routine. As he prepared for his final set, he called attention to us. Since we had the "special" tickets, we were placed in front and center of the audience just below the stage. He then revealed a cafeteria sized table that was covered with a variety of common grocery items.

The man then announced that he was going to tell our story even though he had just met us. Using puns with every item on the table, he told a story of a young girl and boy who fell in love and got married and lived happily ever after. As he said the name of each product, he threw it at us! For example, when he said, "This is your life!" he tossed a large box of Life cereal at us. When he talked about the highs and lows of our relationship, he said, "The tide goes in and comes back out," and he threw a regular sized box of Tide detergent at us. This continued until Ron and I had every single grocery item from the table—including toilet paper!

Tithing, Tide, & Toilet Paper

Cling to Christ for the Ride of Your Life!

There's No Way!
If God truly owns everything, how do you feel about giving back to God the first tenth of what He has given to you?

Know His Way!

> ***"Bring the whole tithe into the storehouse, that there may be food in my house. Test me in this," says the LORD Almighty, "and see if I will not throw open the floodgates of heaven and pour out so much blessing that there will not be room enough to store it."*** Malachi 3:10

> ***Each of you should give what you have decided in your heart to give, not reluctantly or under compulsion, for God loves a cheerful giver.*** 2 Corinthians 9:7

> ***You are worthy, our Lord and God, to receive glory and honor and power, for you created all things, and by your will they were created and have their being.*** Revelation 4:11

Tithing, Tide, & Toilet Paper

Write your own *KNOW HIS WAY!*

No Way!

Briefly write your own faithful giving story with the simple pattern below. If your story is unfinished, leave those portions blank:

Before (There's no way!):

During (Know His way!):

After (No way!):

Marshmallows, Pecan Pie, and the Trucks

Topics covered: *Stewardship, God's provision, patience, and power of prayer*

Sometimes God creatively hides a gift for us to find, and sometimes we aren't even looking! Ron graduated from UCF and landed a great job right away. We were still recovering from the costs of college, but we were on our way out of the financial pit where we had lingered for so long. One of the greatest gifts my husband brought to our marriage was his ability to repair just about every part of any vehicle. Since we had no garage, Ron regularly worked on car parts, and other projects, in our tiny kitchen and living room. *The man is a genius!* Each time the junk yard would call out to our automobiles, my husband would resurrect them yet again.

Bill paying had become much more comfortable, and we actually had enough surplus to start saving for a more dependable vehicle. Ron and I agreed on a Chevy Silverado pick-up truck with a full bench seat in the back. We planned to have it for a long time, and it had enough room for four future kids. It would have to be a used truck to stick to our price range, though. We both enjoyed dreaming about the day when we finally had enough money saved.

One Christmas as we headed to Georgia in our bouncy, four-wheel drive Toyota pick-up truck, it suddenly gave out in a big way right around dinner time. We pulled over to a small gas station with a sub shop next door. It was filthy beyond anything I have ever seen before or since, and they had no soap! There was no way that we were going to eat there, and they did not have any pre-packaged food that was "safe" to eat. Our attitudes were sour, to say the least. With our tummies rumbling and our truck in need of some obscure part, we decided to accept our fate and stay the night at the motel next door. There was nothing else in sight. We used the hotel phone to check in with family about our delay and to ask for their prayers.

Ron worked on the truck, ordered the part he needed, and we unloaded our bicycles from the back. Breaking highway rules, we rode our bikes on the shoulder of the road to the next exit. This was much further on bicycle than expected, especially in the dead of winter, but there was a small "greasy spoon" type café nearby with *clean* bathrooms. We were finally able to eat dinner before biking back to the hotel.

Ron continued to try to repair the truck through the bitter cold night, but the job was too big to conquer in a motel parking lot with such limited time and resources. He then researched renting a car, so that we wouldn't miss Christmas altogether. This small town only had a couple of rental cars, which were already claimed, but they expected one to return late the following afternoon.

Once we checked out of the motel, we had nowhere to go with our luggage and bicycles in the chill of December. The marshmallows and pecan pie intended for our Christmas festivities became our only source of nutrition. While the marshmallows sufficed, the pie was terribly stale after sitting so long in the broken down truck. At least we had food. Not only that, but we just happened to have brought our mountain bikes with us on this trip.

We somehow got all of our belongings to the small car lot where the rental car was expected to arrive several hours later. The gentleman working there was very kind and allowed us to "park" our luggage off in a corner as we just killed time. We visited and played games and made the best of it. Our vacation photos from that afternoon still bring back sweet memories.

After warming up inside, we strolled out to the car lot just to look around. *How funny!* Our Chevy Silverado dream truck just happened to be out there among the small selection of vehicles. It was even blue. It was so pretty. It had no price listed. We both knew our magic number that we could afford, and we were certain this beautiful truck would be far above it.

Out of curiosity, Ron asked the salesman the price. Now, this man knew that we were out of cash, and that we were just biding our time until that car rental showed up; so, he spouted off a number without thinking. This was not just any number, it was *the* number! We looked at each other in shock.

"We'll take it!"

The poor man was flustered beyond belief. "What?"

"We'll take it!"

"But…but…"

He then explained how he had just gotten that truck from the previous owner, who had bought it brand new, and he hadn't really even looked at the blue book value yet. We waited for him to figure out what he was going to do. We could not afford to pay any more. *He agreed!*

Before that rental car ever showed up, we loaded up into our new dream truck and headed to the nearest drive-through to celebrate! We could hardly believe the gift God had given to us! '*Tis so sweet to trust in Jesus!* Twenty years and six kids later, we still have that sweet, old, rusty, dream truck.

Marshmallows, Pecan Pie, and the Trucks

Cling to Christ for the Ride of Your Life!

There's No Way!
What actions can you take to better seek the sweetness in sour situations?

Know His Way!

> ***Know also that wisdom is like honey for you: If you find it, there is a future hope for you, and your hope will not be cut off.*** Proverbs 24:14
>
> ***But seek first his kingdom and his righteousness, and all these things will be given to you as well.*** Matthew 6:33
>
> ***Wait for the LORD; be strong and take heart and wait for the LORD.*** Psalm 27:14

Marshmallows, Pecan Pie, and the Trucks

Write your own *KNOW HIS WAY!*

No Way!

Briefly write your own sour to sweet story with the simple pattern below. If your story is unfinished, leave those portions blank:

Before (There's no way!):

During (Know His way!):

After (No way!):

Only for a Year (or Six)

Topics covered: *Moving, leaving family, marriage, fellowship of believers, church, small groups, God's timing, and God's provision*

After less than a year at his new job, my husband was offered the "deal of a lifetime." The company proposed to send us to southern California for a one-year assignment. During that time, Ron would earn per diem allowing us to save up to buy our first house when we returned. Was this God's plan? How could we leave our families? We were all so close. We prayed for God to clearly show us His direction.

That spring, we were flown out to the Antelope Valley to scope out the offer and deliver our final answer. Although we searched for a rental house, and I interviewed for a teaching position, it was most important to us to find a church home. That would confirm if this move was God's will.

During the week, we went horse-back riding and snow-skiing, and all of our meals and traveling expenses were fully covered. It was an incredible opportunity and a super vacation! Then, on Wednesday of that week, we left a phone message at the office of a local church to find out if they had a mid-week Bible study of some kind. Within one hour, three different people had called our hotel room to invite us to three different small groups! We were impressed! What a warm welcome!

We decided to visit the first family who had called. There were only a few couples at the Bible study that night, but we felt as though they were our life-long friends. Never before had we connected so closely with other Christian couples. Afterward, Ron and I whole-heartedly agreed that the Antelope Valley was our new home. Little did we know that it would be our home for the next six years, which would hold some of our sweetest memories. The distance from our own families would force us as a couple to cling to Christ and each other, strengthening our relationship beyond our comprehension.

Only for a Year (or Six)

Cling to Christ for the Ride of Your Life!

There's No Way!
What would it take for you to be willing to go wherever and whenever God leads you?

Know His Way!

> ***The LORD had said to Abram, "Go from your country, your people and your father's household to the land I will show you. … So Abram left, as the LORD had told him***
> Genesis 12:1, 4a

> ***Then Jesus said to his disciples, "Whoever wants to be my disciple must deny themselves and take up their cross and follow me.*** Matthew 16:24

> ***Direct me in the path of your commands, for there I find delight.*** Psalm 119:35

Only for a Year (or Six)

Write your own *KNOW HIS WAY!*

No Way!

Using the simple pattern below, briefly write your own story about moving out of your comfort zone. If your story is unfinished, leave those portions blank:

Before (There's no way!):

During (Know His way!):

After (No way!):

Why Did I Mail That?
I Can't Get it Back!

Topics covered: *Power of prayer, immediate obedience, sharing prayer requests and answered prayers, and fertility.*

My husband and I had been praying heavily for a young, married couple at our church. They so deeply wanted to have a baby! Each previous hope had resulted in painful disappointment. They were heart-broken, and we were heart-broken for them. One Saturday, I had been particularly crying out to God for my friends, and I suddenly felt absolutely sure that they were going to have a baby. I was *so* sure, in fact, that I wrote a note on a little card telling them, and I immediately mailed it.

As I released the envelope into our community mailbox, my heart sank along with it. *What did I just do?* They had been through so much! *What if I was wrong?* There was no way to retrieve it! I was frustrated with God for allowing me to act so rashly!

I told my husband what I had done and fretted over how to handle it. He suggested that I talk to the couple the next day at church, since the mail wouldn't be delivered on Sunday, anyway. Maybe, I could just ask them not to open the envelope, so I could spare them the hurt of an empty promise. Thankfully, I had a moment to catch them off by themselves as they first arrived. I nervously explained that I had mailed them a card that said something I wish I hadn't said. Of course, now they were curious. I finally just blurted out the whole story and apologized.

As I told her what I had written, her face broke into a sweet smile. She was so forgiving—or so I thought. With tears in her eyes, she then told me that she was pregnant, but she and her husband had not yet told anyone else. Several months later, their miracle baby was born healthy and strong and cute as could be! *How could I have ever doubted?*

Why Did I Mail That? I Can't Get it Back!

Cling to Christ for the Ride of Your Life!

There's No Way!

When are you most likely to doubt God?

Know His Way!

> ***Immediately Jesus reached out his hand and caught him. "You of little faith," he said, "why did you doubt?"*** Matthew 14:31
>
> ***Immediately the boy's father exclaimed, "I do believe; help me overcome my unbelief!"*** Mark 9:24
>
> ***My sheep listen to my voice; I know them, and they follow me.*** John 10:27

Why Did I Mail That?
I Can't Get it Back!

Write your own ***K<u>NO</u>W HIS <u>WAY!</u>***

No Way!

Using the simple pattern below, briefly write your own story about doubting God's direction. If your story is unfinished, leave those portions blank:

Before (There's no way!):

During (Know His way!):

After (No way!):

I Don't Know Her, But I'm Praying

Topics covered: *Connections between Christians, power of prayer, God's healing, relationships, friends, and marriage*

The lady in my Sunday school class begged us not to forget her prayer request. Her coworker and friend desperately needed to mend her broken marriage and reunite with her family. This request was adamantly repeated each and every week that summer when our two small groups were combined. Once fall began, we moved back to our regular classrooms, and I no longer heard that faithful plea for her friend. I could not forget. I had written it in my prayer journal that first day and prayed for that girl and her marriage every week since.

Several months later, Ron and I met a new couple who had recently joined the adult choir. We all hit it off immediately. Our conversations were filled with laughter. A few weeks after we announced that we were expecting our third child, they discovered that they were expecting their fourth.

As accountability partners, we "prego" mamas joined a small local gym together. This was the start of a close and special friendship. We worked vigorously at the gym, and then took our kids next door to the donut shop. One chocolate covered donut was our routine reward for working so hard. Not many friends would be willing to do that three days a week!

For my birthday, the couple fixed up their house like a quaint restaurant and served my husband and me as though we were dining alone. Our children loved spending time together, too, and we invited the family into our baby-sitting co-op. They soon developed close friendships with our other friends. We were so blessed to know such wonderful people while we lived in California.

Six months after our baby was born, we were scheduled to move back to Florida. We planned our last get together visits with friends before the big day arrived. As I sat with my sweet exercise buddy at her house, she casually mentioned how thankful she was for her coworker who had so many people praying for her a while back. My friend mentioned that coworker by name.

"*What?*" I blurted out. I was so confused, and she did not understand my reaction. She thought I knew her story, but I didn't. She told me that she and her husband had just recently shared their testimony in front of the church, but I had missed it. She then revealed her complete story—the testimony of how God had mended her broken marriage and reunited her with her family! *Our prayers had been answered!*

I Don't Know Her, But I'm Praying

Cling to Christ for the Ride of Your Life!

There's No Way!

What actions will you take to remember to pray regularly for others?

Who will you ask to faithfully pray for your urgent requests?

Know His Way!

> ***Therefore confess your sins to each other and pray for each other so that you may be healed. The prayer of a righteous person is powerful and effective.*** James 5:16

> ***Then you will call on me and come and pray to me, and I will listen to you. You will seek me and find me when you seek me with all your heart.*** Jeremiah 29:12-13

> ***Two are better than one, because they have a good return for their labor: If either of them falls down, one can help the other up. But pity anyone who falls and has no one to help them up.*** Ecclesiastes 4:9-10

I Don't Know Her, But I'm Praying

Write your own *KNOW HIS WAY!*

No Way!

Using the simple pattern below, briefly write your own story about a shared prayer request that was answered. If your story is unfinished, leave those portions blank:

Before (There's no way!):

During (Know His way!):

After (No way!):

Delivery from a Deadly Dime

Topics covered: *Godly intervention, healing, protection, provision, body of believers, power of prayer, and God's timing*

It was moving day—the day we would leave California to drive back to Florida! Helpers had been bustling busily to empty the house until only the heavy pool table remained. In celebration of our completion, we cleared the area and watched as the professional movers heaved the top of the pool table onto its side to fit down the hallway. As they did, a lonely dime dropped out onto the floor underneath, echoing throughout the emptiness onto the tile below. Not willing to risk getting in the way of the straining muscles of men, my husband and I both waited for them to fully exit before attempting to rescue the coin from the anticipated mischievous moves of our two year old daughter.

As soon as the men left the room, Ron went for the dime. *Where was it?* Smiling proudly our toddler, Lisa, had a tale-tale twinkle in her eye.

"Where is the dime?" my husband asked.

I immediately went to the bouncy seat where our six month old sputtered. *Oh no!*

"What did you do with the dime?" Ron demanded as calmly as possible.

"I put it in her mouth," she answered sweetly.

By then, I had already picked up the baby, instinctively turned her over, and patted her back until she was breathing freely. She was still complaining, but seemed to be fine. I called our pediatrician to find out what I should do next.

Because the coin was so small, it was highly possible that she simply swallowed it and would pass it through her digestive system; however, because *she* was so small, they could not be sure that it would not lodge somewhere along the way. The nurse told me not to feed her *anything* and to bring her to the emergency clinic across the street from the hospital. Kara was already very hungry, so I was anxious to get the approval to feed her. The moving truck would have to leave without us.

There was still much to be done in order for our own pick-up truck to be completely packed; so, we agreed that Ron should stay to finish loading up while I took Kara in another vehicle. Our friends all pitched in to help. One family took our four year old and two year old to their house to play. Others stayed to help Ron with the last details of the house.

Before I could leave, I needed assistance with adjusting the car seat. Our baby girl had just outgrown her infant carrier, and our friends had given us a toddler style car seat, which we had not yet used. It was rather plush and had different reclining positions on it. Since Kara did not yet sit well on her own, the seat was supposed to completely lay down facing the rear of the car. Two men and I all fought furiously with that stubborn car seat, but not one of us could get it to move out of the forward-most position. She would just have to sit straight up for the twenty minute drive to the clinic.

We prayed together, and I drove by myself with one hand on my little girl's chubby face the whole time making sure she was still breathing. I could not see her. She sucked on my fingers fussing just enough to let me know that she would prefer mommy's milk. The clinic was packed. It was obvious that we were not considered an urgent case once my happy-go-lucky baby smiled preciously at the nurse who signed us in. Hunger could not compete with the other ailments in the room.

This was my third daughter. I had breast fed every one of them, and I knew if I laid her back that she would assume it was finally meal time. With our stroller already packed at home, I had to hold her upright for hours. She had had enough. She was ravenous and exhausted, and so was I. My arm muscles burned from holding her continually for the past few hours standing up.

I begged the nurse to find me a place somewhere in the clinic where I could at least let her lie down. Glad to have some peace in the waiting area, she found an unused room where I could sit and possibly lay the baby down on the paper covered examination table. She reminded me not to feed her—*as though I would forget!* As soon as she closed the door behind her, my tears trickled out. I cried out to God in prayer.

In a matter of minutes my sweet baby fell asleep soundly enough that I could at last lay her back in my arms. When I did, her face turned blue in a matter of seconds. I sat her upright again, and the color returned to her face. I yanked on the emergency cord in the room and a nurse came right in. She had me lay her down on the table to check her, but when I laid Kara back, she immediately stopped breathing and blue crept over her face again. I picked her up and patted her back. She cried--so did I.

We suddenly became the most urgent condition in the clinic. I was escorted to the x-ray room. In order to film the location of the lodged dime, Kara would have to be laid down for a moment. I dreaded the predictable blue I would see one more time, yet I could not take my eyes off of her precious face. As expected, the dime was toggling at the top of her windpipe closing it off only if she was lying down. She would need a surgical procedure to remove it.

I called to update my husband. He was racing to tie up the last few loose ends in order to meet me at the hospital, but Kara was already scheduled to prepare for surgery as soon I could get her to the emergency room. I was crumbling. We prayed together, and I once more placed my baby in the upright car seat and buckled her in to drive across the street. I was greeted by medical staff who whisked us down the hall and began the necessary paperwork.

Before driving to the hospital, my husband had quickly called our friends to share our urgent prayer request. My friend's husband was fairly close to the hospital, so he dropped everything to wait at the hospital with me until Ron could arrive. At the sight of a familiar face, I fell apart. They had already taken Kara to prepare her for the anesthesia. I was so afraid.

Within a few hours, Kara had recovered, and the doctor handed us the fateful dime. I was encouraged to feed her for the first time in over twelve hours. With my baby in my arms, I poured out my praise and thanksgiving to God for delivering us all through such an eventful day and night. Once released from the hospital, we snuggled our sleepy baby girl into her car seat. This time, when we pulled the knobs to recline the seat, it smoothly settled back as though nothing had ever been wrong. It never got stuck again.

Delivery from a Deadly Dime

Cling to Christ for the Ride of Your Life!

There's No Way!

If you believe that God already knows your life story, how can you better line up your plans with His?

Know His Way!

> ***He has delivered us from such a deadly peril, and he will deliver us again. On him we have set our hope that he will continue to deliver us,*** 2 Corinthians 1:10
>
> ***Even though I walk through the darkest valley, I will fear no evil, for you are with me; your rod and your staff, they comfort me.*** Psalm 23:4
>
> ***Why, you do not even know what will happen tomorrow. What is your life? You are a mist that appears for a little while and then vanishes. Instead, you ought to say, "If it is the Lord's will, we will live and do this or that."***
> James 4:14-15

Delivery from a Deadly Dime

Write your own *K**NO**W HIS **WAY!***

No Way!

Using the simple pattern below, briefly write your own story about God's deliverance through a fearful experience. If your story is unfinished, leave those portions blank:

Before (There's no way!):

During (Know His way!):

After (No way!):

Two Years: Five Moves, Three Jobs, and a Baby

Topics covered: *Difficult times, moving, job loss, provision, valleys of life, struggles, integrity, and extended family*

While in transit from the west coast to the east coast, our time was limited. My husband had to report for his new job on a certain day, and thanks to my two year old feeding her baby sister a dime on moving day, we were behind schedule. That week-long drive was extensive, but it was also filled with periodic sweet brief stops to see a few sights and family. Our focus began to shift from all that we had left behind to all that we would face ahead.

Although our move was paid for by the company, Ron took a significant pay cut by accepting this new position. We were leaving the first home we had ever purchased to move into a much smaller temporary apartment. The painful separation from our friends and church family was softened by the exciting anticipation that we would live closer to our relatives. We would reside just over an hour away from all of my family in Florida and only a day's drive from all of Ron's family in Georgia. This adventure differed greatly from the one that had led us to California in the first place. We now had three young daughters, and we had two places to genuinely call home. *What would it take for us to feel settled again?*

After a short hotel stay, we found a tiny furnished condominium right across the street from the beach! It was dusty and old, but perfect until we could find something more permanent. Three months later, we found our church and our rental home—with a pool! Finally we enjoyed the fellowship of other believers once again and began to develop new endearing friendships. In addition, my dad moved nearby from out of state.

His regular visits bonded my kids with their Gramps and me with my dad.

During that year and a half, Ron accepted a completely different job, which allowed him to work from home. It required an enormous amount of weekly travel. Just after the birth of our fourth daughter, we were notified that our landlord needed to move back into her home right away. After much prayer, our next move took us an hour away from my dad and our church home, but much closer to my mom and sisters. This home owner verbally agreed to let us rent month to month after our initial six month lease. This meant we only had one move left before we could be settled at last. It seemed too good to be true!

Since Ron traveled so often, we had very limited time together. We spent that precious time eagerly shopping for a permanent house and a church home. Fervently praying for God to show us the home He had prepared for us, we willingly opened up our expectations to accept whatever He delivered. At one point, we bid simultaneously on several houses, figuring we would just take the bid we won, but every single offer fell through. We worked with a patient and diligent realtor, who called us one day ecstatic to announce that he had found our dream home. He really had!

As time slipped by while we had been desperately house hunting, a brand new neighborhood in the middle of nowhere had opened up. We already knew the builder had a model that was truly the house of our dreams, but it exceeded our price range—until now! Because the location was not yet developed, the price was *exactly* our agreed upon amount. We had our pick of the lot. It was far above anything we had imagined we could afford! Our God had been lavishly generous with us yet again.

With four months left before our expected final move day, Ron walked outside of our rental home to find a surprising "For Sale" sign in the front yard and a lockbox on the front door. He immediately called the landlord, who explained that she needed to sell the house right away; so, she had given her realtor permission to show it around the clock. Our own possessions were still in boxes stored sky high in every closet ready for our next move; so, there wasn't even a place to "shove" the daily toys and clutter that first day when strangers showed up unannounced. I arrived home from the grocery store to find people inspecting every nook and cranny of the house. With four daughters ages seven and under and my husband out of town on weekdays, it was unnerving.

After establishing ground rules, realtors still showed the house several times each day. I had a nursing infant, a potty-training toddler, and two children to homeschool, and while I agreed to cooperate to show the home, the constant disruption and impending sale prompted us to seek another option. After heavy daily prayer, Ron and I accepted his parents' sincere offer to move in with them in Georgia. We gave our notice and moved the following month. Just as we had expected, the house sold before our new home was ready. We had made the right decision.

Now, most people cringe when I tell about moving in with my in-laws, but the next four months were to be the answer to many different prayers. Once our belongings were again in storage, we settled into the peaceful, supportive comfort of our new home with family. Unanimously we agreed to treat the situation as though we were roommates. We could maintain our own family routines, purchase our own groceries, and take care of our own meals unless we planned otherwise. It worked beautifully!

Ron traveled out of Atlanta during the week and joined us for the weekends. I was no longer alone feeling stranded while he traveled. We fell into an immediate routine to homeschool and exercise, and I even joined a local Bible study. Knowing that our hopefully final move was just around the bend, we thoroughly enjoyed the oasis in the midst of our desert of wandering. Our families bonded incredibly. What a blessing to love and be loved! Just one month prior to our trek back to Florida for the closing of our house, we sat surrounded by family and watched with horror the attack of 9-11. It was with deeply mixed emotions that we parted in mid-October as we now had yet another state to call "home."

In just a few months, as a result of the unsteady market, the company Ron worked for closed. We faced the reality that we could not afford to stay in our brand new home unless he found another solid job fairly soon. With God's perfect timing, he quickly landed the perfect position! Only fifteen minutes from our house, my husband would have regular hours, very little travel, and the income to pay the bills. *Our two year season of wandering had finally come to an end!*

Two Years: Five Moves, Three Jobs, and a Baby

Cling to Christ for the Ride of Your Life!

There's No Way!

What actions can you take to help someone who is in the midst of a season of trials?

Know His Way!

> ***For the LORD is good and his love endures forever; his faithfulness continues through all generations.*** Psalm 100:5
>
> ***Consider it pure joy, my brothers and sisters, whenever you face trials of many kinds, because you know that the testing of your faith produces perseverance.*** James 1:2-3
>
> ***But in keeping with his promise we are looking forward to a new heaven and a new earth, where righteousness dwells.*** 2 Peter 3:13

Two Years: Five Moves, Three Jobs, and a Baby

Write your own ***K<u>NO</u>W HIS <u>WAY!</u>***

No Way!

Using the simple pattern below, briefly write your own story about a season of trials in your life. If your story is unfinished, leave those portions blank:

Before (There's no way!):

During (Know His way!):

After (No way!):

Penny-Pinching and Provisions

Topics covered: *Provision, power of prayer, God's creativity, family, and babies*

Ever since God so creatively provided our groceries using a secular comedian, we knew He was trustworthy to provide for all of our needs, even if His timing was not the same as ours. It has become a common joke in our household that if I happen to mention, "Wouldn't it be nice to have (something)," then that "something" will miraculously come our way by surprise. Do not misunderstand me; I am not referring to a "genie in a bottle" type of request for wealth and riches. I am talking about what some would consider "needs" and others would consider "wants." These particular provisions we could have lived without, but God chose to bless us with them anyway. Some of them we prayed for. Others I just happened to mention while dreaming out loud. All of them were confirmations of God's grace and generosity. Oh, how He loves us!

***

After our dogs destroyed our only couches, we received a beautiful living room set from my sister, which moved with us numerous times. In order not to store it, we gave it away during one of our moves, and another sister surprised us with her couch set at the new home. For the other sitting area, my husband was hoping for a tan leather couch, and we decided to wait for it. Sure enough, one day while sitting on the floor of that room with a friend, she asked me if we would like a couch for it, because she and her husband were giving one away. Not knowing our taste, she said that we might not like it. It was a tan, leather couch!

***

One evening my husband and I sat down to an at home movie date night. Seeing that the entertainment center was leaning to one side, I gave it a shove before sitting down for the show. Without giving it much thought, I casually told my husband that I would love to one day have an armoire like the one my sister had. The next morning our neighborhood was bustling with a community yard sale. We traditionally only visit the homes in our cul-de-sac, and I typically find something I like at one house in particular. This year was no different. The exact armoire I had mentioned the night before was soon moved in to replace the rickety leaning tower of entertainment.

***

Because we have moved so many, many times, we are especially sensitive to others who are under the burden of a move. My husband is the king of packing a storage unit or a moving truck to its fullest, and he has helped to move more people than I could possibly count. During one of these helps, the owners decided that they no longer wanted their ugly, faded orangey-red topped pool table. *Go figure!* Ron and I were both so excited to have the pool table that we didn't care about the nasty color.

A few years later, as the moving company unloaded all of our furniture from the long route from California to Florida, only one thing had been destroyed. The orangey-red felt was shredded to pieces. As they apologized and assured us that the insurance would completely repair the damage and even replace all of the bumpers, we rejoiced. Burgundy felt would look beautiful!

***

The somewhat surprise of our fifth daughter brought on one provision that demanded attention. We would no longer be able to fit our whole family into our six seat pick-up truck. My detail oriented husband began his research for our next vehicle. Ron found the perfect Suburban, but it was in another state, and we did not quite have enough money to buy it. He continued his search. Three months before the baby was born, we received a shocking enormous gift: a Ford Taurus. My dad and stepmom had decided to scale down to just one vehicle, and they gave us their car! We were told to use it however it would best help us; so, we sold it and used the money to buy Ron a one way plane ticket and to purchase our much-loved Suburban.

***

There is a mysterious phase of life in which women seem to suddenly swarm to help one another. The announcement of a pregnancy brings it on in a flash, and instantly those who have "been there and done that" seek to help those who are innocently treading on new ground. I have watched this miracle happen repeatedly. From maternity clothes to postpartum outfits and from baby clothes to all the other baby paraphernalia, someone somewhere has something to share.

The area in which we have received the most unsolicited provision is definitely baby related. With my first child, I was handed bags of maternity clothes and baby clothes before I even had time to realize that I needed them. Without hinting to anyone that I needed anything, everything was provided for every one of my babies. After five girls and the announcement of my expected boy, the bags of boy clothes in all different sizes and from various people were greatly appreciated. As I sorted through to see what I still needed, I discovered that I had every single size of boy clothes newborn to 3T.

***

Although we have always had our basic necessities taken care of, we have many times stretched from paycheck to paycheck to make the groceries last just a little bit longer. One morning in December I woke up a bit later with my kids, since it was not a school day. When I opened up the fridge, it was completely empty, except for condiments and several cans of soda from a previous Christmas party. Our pantry was just as scarce. I did not even have the ingredients to piece something together. *Ugh.* With the costs of Christmas time, I was really hoping to make it to pay day.

The kids and I laughed about our potential breakfast of soda and condiments, and then we gathered around to pray for God to show us what to do. As we finished our prayer, the doorbell rang. At the front door step was a large package, which said to open it right away. How exciting! We brought it to the table while all eyes searched to see who had sent it, but there was no name on it other than our own. Inside was the largest box of Hickory Farms holiday food that I have ever seen. It had four small roasts, an abundance of cheeses, sausages, dried fruits, cakes, nuts, and candies. It was enough to feed our family for the rest of the two days until pay day! Many weeks later, an old friend of my husband's came over for dinner and games, and he asked us how we liked the food he had sent. We ran to show him the pictures of the empty fridge and pantry and the feast we had received. We were so appreciative!

***

Have we received everything we ever asked for? No way! Is God like a genie and my wish is His command? Absolutely not! Although Jesus came to serve, we are His servants. He lovingly gives us the desires of our hearts when we delight ourselves in Him. When my family is tempted to worry about provision, we remember the multitude of times when the Lord has provided above and beyond our expectations. He has brought us beds, dressers, groceries (many times), car seats, strollers, baby swings, bouncy seats, baby monitors, a playpen, bassinet, high chair, clothes, shoes, sport supplies, bicycles, and much, much more. It is important to note that often God utilized our church and extended family to supply our needs. He has also used us to provide for others. His power has no limits. He is a creative and generous God!

Penny-Pinching and Provisions

Cling to Christ for the Ride of Your Life!

There's No Way!

Since your heavenly Father knows what you need, are you willing to seek God's righteousness first and to pray with thanksgiving?

Which provisions are you most likely to worry about?

Know His Way!

> ***Give us today our daily bread.*** Matthew 6:11
>
> ***Therefore I tell you, do not worry about your life, what you will eat or drink; or about your body, what you will wear. Is not life more than food, and the body more than clothes? …your heavenly Father knows that you need them. But seek first his kingdom and his righteousness, and all these things will be given to you as well.*** Matthew 6:25, 32b, 33
>
> ***Do not be anxious about anything, but in every situation, by prayer and petition, with thanksgiving, present your requests to God. And the peace of God, which transcends all understanding, will guard your hearts and your minds in Christ Jesus.*** Philippians 4:6-7

Penny-Pinching and Provisions

Write your own *KNOW HIS WAY!*

No Way!

Using the simple pattern below, briefly write your own story about receiving a needed (or wanted) item in a way that shows God's gracious generosity. If your story is unfinished, leave those portions blank:

Before (There's no way!):

During (Know His way!):

After (No way!):

Instruments of God

Topics covered: *Power of prayer, God's gifts, provision, God's timing, and music*

Music has always played a huge part in my life. It is truly one of my very favorite gifts from God. Honestly, I do not remember a time when I have not had the pleasure of music. The eldest of my three sisters taught us to sing our first complete song in harmony on a long car ride to an audition, and that began a sweet season of memories. We performed as "The Freeman Sisters" mostly for local entertainment in the area surrounding our home town. The practices were difficult, but the bonding and laughter we shared made it all worth it. In addition, we each dove into every other possible musical opportunity we could find.

After praying to accept the free gift of life through Jesus, His Spirit lived inside of me, and I discovered a passion to worship the Lord in song. My husband and I enjoyed singing together in various church ministries for many years. As a result, it was only natural to share these praise songs and hymns as nightly lullabies to our babies. To this day, I still regularly sing my children to sleep while scratching their backs. Our kids each have an enormous love for music, too. It is part of who we are as a family.

***

Although my sisters and I had experienced musical performance with acting and singing, we never learned how to play an instrument. My husband had played piano as a child and almost three years of guitar as a teen, but had not pursued either one. At the age of six, our first daughter desperately wanted to play guitar. A year later, since her desire was only stronger, we followed through with her first Baby Taylor acoustic guitar and weekly lessons. *She was in love!* The move to our newly built home took us over an hour away from Amy's guitar teacher, and the search for a replacement was delayed by my husband's job loss. While we were disappointed, we also trusted that God would provide at the right time and in the right way if He intended for her to learn.

A few years later, we discovered, quite by accident, that my husband's close friend lived with his family in the neighborhood across the road from ours. This man had been in our wedding, but the guys had lost touch over the years. As friends often do, they picked up right where they had left off. He offered Ron free regular guitar lessons for Amy, which combined, of course, with catch up visits with her daddy. What a gift! He taught her well enough that she joined a church band, which further fueled her passion for music. She is pursuing a career in musical performance and worship. *God provided perfectly!*

***

Our second eldest daughter dreamed of playing the violin, promising God that she would use it to bring praise to Him. In keeping with tradition, we waited a full year to ensure that this was not just a fickle notion. The following year, she received her first violin, and her new music instructor lived at the end of our street. Lisa could easily walk to and from lessons while I continued to school the other children. We dearly loved the teacher, but later needed a financial breather from lessons. During that time, Lisa shared her desire to play fiddle, instead of classical violin. God would have to provide once again, if it was His plan.

Some time later, a friend invited us to visit a group of folks who gather to play blue grass music. They perform throughout the area and regularly enjoy jam sessions in various members' homes. At the first meeting, Ron and Amy brought their guitars and Lisa brought her fiddle. *They had a blast!* They were quickly taken in by the regulars and shown the ropes. Amy played a mandolin for the first time, and Lisa played on a fiddle that was over one hundred years old. The girls returned home with huge smiles and the gift of a musical soundtrack for every song that the group plays. After a second visit and a great deal of practice, Lisa has perfected her fiddle playing! *God provided once again!*

***

Since then, Lisa outgrew her violin, and began to save for a full size. At her sister's high school graduation party, the man who had taught Amy guitar arrived with his family. As our family members mingled with the guests, we were made two unique offers simultaneously by the man and his wife. Noticing our only room yet in need of an area rug, he told me that he might have one for it. No one had said anything to him, but that same morning I had rearranged furniture and had mentioned the need for another rug.

At the same time that he was offering me the rug, his wife was offering the use of her full size violin to Lisa until she saved enough for her own. Her husband had recently purchased one for her to play in the church orchestra, and he had completely refurbished her original. This was no small offer. This violin held great sentiment. What a sacrificial gift! He left the party just long enough to fetch the violin and the rug. The carpet looked like it was made for that exact spot in our house, and Lisa has relished in the enjoyment of playing such a beautiful instrument.

***

Our third daughter, Kara, chose a drum set as her instrument, which she received as a gift one year after her initial request. She had saved diligently for half of the cost and played on a makeshift set in the mean time. When her first teacher moved away, her second instructor moved in next door to us. This was another perfect blend for our homeschool schedule.

During her second year of lessons, Kara listed a “ride cymbal” on her birthday wish list. I did not know what kind to get, and her teacher was not available to ask right away; so, I asked Ron’s buddy who had taught Amy to play guitar. He and his family were at our house when I inquired about the best place to purchase one. Wryly, he answered that he knew *exactly* where I could get one. Later that same day he returned with a shiny ride cymbal, which he had been storing. *It was just what Kara had hoped for!*

***

Our fourth daughter, Angie, saved her money and paid half for an upscale keyboard that we found at a moving sale. Naturally generous at heart, she has sweetly shared the instrument with each of her siblings. The beauty of having a keyboard verses a piano is the option to use headphones. In a house filled with people around the clock, this is a definite plus; however, once Amy began college music classes, a full size piano with pedals and weighted keys became a necessity.

This was financially out of our reach. Even when a friend advertised by email the sale of her upright grand, we simply could not do it. I did not even tell anyone that we were interested. When her family was given a beautiful couch, she called me. She wanted to pass on the blessing by giving us her piano. We had never told her that we needed a piano in the first place. *Apparently, God had.*

***

Within the very same week that we received the piano, my family joined my mom, her two brothers, and their wives for dessert. We had a sweet time listening to my uncles and my mom as they shared their childhood memories. They reminisced about days when they had made ice cream for dinner and enjoyed their dad's drum playing. We all were tickled as my one uncle played a real key chain sized harmonica.

Having heard that Amy was majoring in music, my other uncle inquired further. She told of her dream to play as many different instruments as possible, and he then offered her a spectacular gift. He and my aunt would be spending half the year up north with their grandkids; so, he suggested that during that time Amy should learn to play his marimba, which he had had since he was sixteen. Additionally, he gave her his original sheet music to use until his return. A banjolin that had been purchased for my mom as a child was also added to the mix. *What an incredible opportunity beyond Amy's wildest dreams!*

***

Relatively speaking, musical instruments are not a necessity--but what enjoyment they bring! They are sprinkled throughout the Bible, God's Holy Word; so, they must be important to Him. With these tools we can give a unique gift of worship to our Creator for His pleasure. Maybe that is why He has so generously shared them with us as His children. *May He receive all the glory, honor, and praise through every instrument He has blessed us with!*

Instruments of God

Cling to Christ for the Ride of Your Life!

There's No Way!

What part does music play in your life?

Know His Way!

> ***Praise the LORD with the harp; make music to him on the ten-stringed lyre.*** Psalm 33:2
>
> ***It is good to praise the LORD and make music to your name, O Most High, proclaiming your love in the morning and your faithfulness at night, to the music of the ten-stringed lyre and the melody of the harp. For you make me glad by your deeds, LORD; I sing for joy at what your hands have done.*** Psalm 92:1-4
>
> ***The trumpeters and musicians joined in unison to give praise and thanks to the LORD. Accompanied by trumpets, cymbals and other instruments, the singers raised their voices in praise to the LORD and sang: "He is good; his love endures forever." Then the temple of the LORD was filled with the cloud, and the priests could not perform their service because of the cloud, for the glory of the LORD filled the temple of God.*** 2 Chronicles 5:13-14

Instruments of God

Write your own *K**NO**W HIS **WAY!***

No Way!

Using the simple pattern below, briefly write your own story about an instrument or tool of God. If your story is unfinished, leave those portions blank:

Before (There's no way!):

During (Know His way!):

After (No way!):

I Really *Was* Blind, But Now I See

Topics covered: *Power of prayer, God's physical healing, laughter, and the importance of testimonies*

People handle the overload of stressful and nervous situations in all sorts of different ways. For my mom and sisters, we have been known, on rare occasions, to get the giggles uncontrollably when it is most inappropriate—which makes us laugh that much harder. Sometimes the hilarity continues until it has turned completely into tears. As a kid, I remember two separate occasions when I was on stage in the midst of a performing choir when the contagion began. The more the choir director stared me down, the less control I had. I tried everything to stop the laughter, but it seemed to take on a will of its own, and the resulting embarrassment could easily cause a flare up once again after I had finally stopped.

One of my most embarrassing moments occurred at an eye doctor appointment. My husband surprised me on *his* birthday with the money to get my first pair of contact lenses. I was so excited! I was also nervous; so, he went into the examination room with me. His chair was positioned behind the doctor and facing me. The optometrist seemed on the serious side, which added to the butterflies in my stomach. Not knowing what to expect, when he suddenly put his face no more than two inches from my face and turned his head from side to side to look into my eye, I felt the giggles coming on. I tried to shove from my mind the thoughts that were flooding in:

"I can actually see his pores."

"Okay, this guy is close enough for me to smell him."

"I bet he can smell my breath with my mouth shut."

"I had better hold my breath." *I did.*

"Oh no…He has a pimple."

At that point, the built up pressure from holding my breath and my laughter all exploded through my tightly pursed lips which unsuccessfully fought to hold it all in. In shock at the sudden spray of laughter, the doctor bolted upright and grabbed a tissue to wipe his face. He was *not* happy!

He then sternly watched me erupt with more laughter, as I apologized profusely in between gasps for air. Just when I began to gain self control, He asked me in all seriousness, "Are you finished?" You can guess what happened. Round two spilled out.

Now the doctor was highly insulted. Ron looked at me with a desperate plea for me to stop, but that only made it worse. Unable to see him, the optometrist whirled around and scolded my husband, thinking he was the cause of my laughter. He then told Ron he would have to leave. I was mortified--so was Ron. With my supposed accomplice out of the room, the doctor attempted again to complete the exam. I chewed my lip hard and focused every ounce of energy on begging God to please help me to completely stop laughing. Somehow we all survived the whole ordeal, and I left that day with contacts. At the follow up appointment we smoothed it all out, and I did not erupt with giggles.

Ever since that particular eye exam, I have warned each consecutive doctor beforehand that I am prone to nervous laughter. Getting this out in the open right up front has prevented a repeat, but remembering that one day can still set me off into side-splitting belly laughs. I have to avoid thinking about it at all costs while having my eyes checked. Years later these memories of laughter from that routine visit would help me through a series of sad and scary eye exams.

During an especially busy season for our family, I developed a large, white blurry blind spot in my vision along with pain, swelling, and intense sensitivity to light. Both of my eyes had been bothering me lately, but I excused it as a lack of sleep. I was extremely run down. No amount of blinking or eye solution would clear the cloudy spot. I searched on the computer, which of course told me that it could be nothing, or I may be about to die from a serious disease.

At the urgent care clinic, I was misdiagnosed with an eye infection called Iritis. The physician was not hopeful that I would see clearly again, and he sent me directly to an emergency ophthalmologist across town. This doctor concurred that scar tissue was indeed the culprit of my loss of vision; however, the cause was not from Iritis. He was unable to determine whether the symptoms were from an allergic reaction to my latest contact solution or possibly from over-wear of my contacts. Regardless of the cause, he could only hope for the dim possibility that the scar tissue may be slightly lessened. As he explained that he was going to attempt a few days of steroid eye drops, he did not mince words. He fully expected that I would never see clearly again. This was basically a "last ditch effort."

During the days ahead as I faithfully used the steroid eye drops as prescribed, the visual blob seemed to disappear, but it was replaced by a new blurriness in both eyes. I could not see with or without my glasses, and I was not allowed to use contacts. I was unable to drive or to function normally as Mom and teacher to my kids. My husband and I and others prayed urgently for a miracle.

I attempted to prepare myself for the gripping news at the follow up appointment with the same emergency ophthalmologist. It had only been a few days, so he remembered me and my case clearly. He did not have much to say as he listened to my admission that my vision was now worse, although the blind spot seemed to be gone. He wanted to see for himself. There was no laughter as I prayed through another eye exam. The doctor wrinkled up his forehead and simply kept saying, "Hmm." He called in a nurse and spoke sternly, but quietly to her; so that I could not hear what he said. She nodded emphatically appearing to be defensive as they looked over my chart.

The physician then continued with the exam, checking my vision, which seemingly became even clearer as we went. Finally, ready to deliver the news, he leaned back and told me that he had no explanation for what had happened to my eyes. *Great!*

He continued: If he had not been the same doctor who had examined my eyes the week before, he would never have believed he was now with the same patient. He had even double-checked with his nurse to be sure that she had the correct chart. Not only was there absolutely no evidence that I had ever had any scar tissue at all, but my vision had improved so significantly that my own glasses were now far over-corrected. This was the cause of the new blurry vision in both eyes. He was completely bewildered, but I told him that I knew God had answered our prayers and healed me. New lens prescriptions with much less correction cleared my vision beautifully.

I Really *Was* Blind, But Now I See

Cling to Christ for the Ride of Your Life!

There's No Way!

How has God used laughter in your life?

What would you most like for God to heal?

Know His Way!

> ***Our mouths were filled with laughter, our tongues with songs of joy. Then it was said among the nations, "The LORD has done great things for them." The LORD has done great things for us, and we are filled with joy.***
> Psalm 126:2-3

> ***The LORD said to him, "Who gave human beings their mouths? Who makes them deaf or mute? Who gives them sight or makes them blind? Is it not I, the LORD?***
> Exodus 4:11

> ***The LORD gives sight to the blind, the LORD lifts up those who are bowed down, the LORD loves the righteous.***
> Psalm 146:8

I Really *Was* Blind, But Now I See

Write your own *KNOW HIS WAY!*

No Way!

Using the simple pattern below, briefly write your own story about healing. If your story is unfinished, leave those portions blank:

Before (There's no way!):

During (Know His way!):

After (No way!):

Fertility May be Futile

Topics covered: *Infertility, fertility, miscarriage, birth control issues, power of prayer, God's promises, and God in control*

Throughout our over twenty years of marriage, my husband and I have been shown repeatedly that God is in control. Our first baby, Amy, was born five years after our wedding. This was not near as soon as we had planned, but the timing was perfect according to God's plan. With our next pregnancy, I had a miscarriage at the end of the first trimester. We were heartbroken. Was it the Lord's plan that we would have one child instead of a house full? As I sought His will, I begged for Him to satisfy the desire of my heart to have another baby.

Psalm 37:4 says, "Delight yourself also in the LORD, and He shall give you the desires of your heart." I had always thought that if I was focused on God then my own heart's desires would be given to me. Hearing the verse over the radio, one day I realized a new meaning. If I delighted in the Lord as the source of my joy, then He would *place* desires within my heart, which He would then fulfill. I questioned myself. Had I truly been seeking joy through God? Yes, I honestly had. An overwhelming peace came over me as I believed wholeheartedly that God had just given me the promise of a baby. I did not know whether it would be by birth or adoption, but I was confident. I claimed Psalm 37:4 as His promise to me, and we chose the name "Lisa" because it means, "God's promise." After an initial meeting with a fertility counselor, we filled out the preliminary charts in preparation for the next month's appointment. Nine months later, Lisa was born.

***

In the same week that my husband and I planned a date night to talk about the possibility of a third baby, we discovered that one was already on the way. When Kara was about a year old, Ron and I again went to dinner with the focus of our conversation on whether or not to have more children. What did the Bible say about it? In *that* very same week, we again discovered that we were already expecting. When Angie was a year old, we decided we had better postpone that talk altogether, seeing as how the answer came so quickly the last two times. We would just wait and pray for clear direction.

***

Our four girls were each about two years apart, and we appreciated this closeness in age, because it facilitated tight friendships. As my youngest approached the age of one and a half, my husband and I addressed the issue of having another baby, but we had no clear answer. Shortly after that conversation, the company Ron worked for closed its doors. Without a job, we felt sure we should wait on our plans to have another child. Once settled at his new job, we prayerfully decided to try for a baby for two months. We both agreed that if we did not conceive during this time, then our family would be complete. The following week, I was injured from a fall while changing the sheets on the kids' top bunk-bed. It took six weeks to heal. According to *our* planned timeline, our baby days were over.

Sometime later, I read a verse one morning that spoke vividly to me. I felt at peace with an assurance that I would eventually have another baby, but not as I had expected and not anytime soon. I wrote these thoughts in my prayer journal to God. My urgent baby yearning ceased. I was truly content. Six months later, during my morning Bible reading and prayers, I read a verse that changed everything. My heart pounded excitedly as I wrote my prayer response to God. Would we really have another baby soon? Sure enough, the following week a test was positive. Remembering the revelation six months prior, I searched through my previous prayer journal to see which verse it was, and what exactly I had written. Tears spilled out as I read the Scripture: Hebrews 11:6. *The very same verse had clearly spoken to me BOTH times!*

***

At the tale-tell ultrasound for our fifth daughter, Lydia, the doctor supposed that we would recognize the blur of body parts. He moved the arrow cursor out of the way so that we could identify what he expected was a familiar sight; however, we thought that the arrow was pointing to the part we were to focus on. Like making out a picture from a cloud, it really could have been anything. He asked with a big smile, "Can you tell?" Rather than just admit that I had no clue what was what, I guessed, "Is it a boy?" Before he could answer, the room was filled with the squeals of my four daughters and I believe my husband wiped a tear from his eye. Flabbergasted, the poor doctor attempted to rewind the moment. "No, no, no! It's a girl!" Stunned silence and confused faces stared at the screen as he showed what was what and apologized for the confusion before the squeals returned at the excitement of another sweet girl.

With three and a half years between our youngest two girls, we wondered if we should just have one more for our littlest to have a playmate. Even numbers seemed easier. Once we knew that we were expecting our sixth baby, we planned our humorous responses to the anticipated remarks that people were sure to blurt out. We had a blast and laughed hysterically at the possible scenarios. This time at the ultrasound, the doctor did not let us guess, and he was ecstatic to tell us that it was a boy. At the birth, our nurse told us that our poor doctor had been stressed all morning about that ultrasound prediction. As he delivered Kaleb, he literally yelled with excitement!

***

Some women just never get over that desire to have another baby. It is how they are made. I am one of them. As I have continued to seek after God with all my heart, though, He has transitioned me to a different phase of my life with the birth of a new ministry. Although I am still subject to get baby fever, those moments no longer linger, pulling at my heart strings as they once did. I have been filled with contentment with so many to love and serve in one household.

We have a few sayings in our home that we quote fairly often. One of them is, “If it’s gray, stay away.” Another one like it is, “If in doubt, do without.” After a great deal of prayer and research, my husband and I could not conclude an absolute clear answer regarding certain means of birth control. Surely, this is how some of our precious children arrived. Having studied the subject matter extensively, we have found extreme opinions on both sides of the fence. Some issues we have resolved, and others remain gray to us. God has already shown us that He could delay a pregnancy while we used no contraceptive, and that He could bless us with a pregnancy while we were using a reliable means of birth control. We only *thought* we had control.

Two months before my forty-first birthday, my youngest daughter diligently prayed every day that God would give mommy twin babies. We were all tickled at her consistency, but within a couple of weeks, I found out unexpectedly that I was pregnant. My husband and I chose to announce it for the sole purpose of much needed prayer support. After the initial shock wore off, we excitedly came up with names for twins, since that was what my daughter had ordered, but sadly I miscarried once again. Why would God have enabled us to conceive and yet allow such devastation for our whole family? I wrestled with the answer, yet clung to Christ. I was comforted to know so many were praying with us through the whole ordeal.

The healing process was long for me, especially. My desire to have and hold another baby or two had been strongly rekindled within me. I struggled to understand what God was up to. My husband and I revisited our search to resolve the issue of permanent means of birth control. Was it our own lack of decision at the source of our situation? As the head of our family who was seeking God daily, I knew that Ron could be trusted as I willingly submitted to his guidance. The morning before our appointment for his vasectomy, I broke down. His parents happened to be staying with us, and we gathered to pray. I told them that I felt as though I was being tested as Abraham had been with Isaac's sacrifice. I was fully willing to obey the Lord, but I just believed that God was somehow going to intervene at the last minute. Ron's dad wisely pointed to a verse on a decoration nearby, "Rest in God alone. ~Psalm 62:1."

We arrived on time to the appointment. We had squeezed into the last week before the New Year, since we could only afford to do this while our deductible had already been met. All the way to the office, Ron and I each counseled with entrusted Christian friends by phone. Were we doing the right thing? We knew that our very closest friends were praying. Ron signed in, but stepped outside of the doors to finish his phone conversation while waiting his turn. With an apologetic expression, the nurse asked to speak with me. She said that she was sorry, but there would be no procedure that day. *What? Why?*

When Ron had signed in, he had mentioned to the nurse that he had a cold. While she did not expect that to make a difference, she said she would check with the doctor just in case. The physician was emphatic that he would not follow through until

Ron was completely healthy, but we could schedule an appointment for the following week. We knew this was not an option because of the new deductible that must be met for the New Year. The nurse again spoke with the doctor to confirm. *God had intervened.*

***

While we do not have plans to try for another baby, long ago we came to grips with the fact that God's ways are not our ways. Thankfully, His plans are always for good. As a Father, He dearly loves His children and wants what is best for us in light of eternity. Knowing that He is the Author of our story, and that He loves us far greater than we even love ourselves, we can rest in His tender mercies and abundant grace. With perfect clarity He sees the big picture of our lives, and He will guide us perfectly when we are tuned in to obey His Word.

Fertility May be Futile

Cling to Christ for the Ride of Your Life!

There's No Way!

What aspect of having children will you entrust to God?

Know His Way!

> ***Take delight in the LORD, and he will give you the desires of your heart.*** Psalm 37:4
>
> ***Children are a heritage from the LORD, offspring a reward from him.*** Psalm 127:3
>
> ***Praise be to the God and Father of our Lord Jesus Christ, the Father of compassion and the God of all comfort, who comforts us in all our troubles, so that we can comfort those in any trouble with the comfort we ourselves receive from God.*** 2 Corinthians 1:3-4
>
> ***And without faith it is impossible to please God, because anyone who comes to him must believe that he exists and that he rewards those who earnestly seek him.*** Hebrews 11:6

Fertility May be Futile

Write your own ***KNOW HIS WAY!***

No Way!

Using the simple pattern below, briefly write your own story about children. If your story is unfinished, leave those portions blank:

Before (There's no way!):

During (Know His way!):

After (No way!):

In Awe of God

Topics covered: *Power of prayer, praising God through story-telling, missions, provision, and Rite of Passage Parenting*

After attending Dr. Walker Moore's moving presentation during the Global Missions Conference at our church, my eldest daughter's announcement did not take me by surprise. She was anxious to experience an Awe Star Mission Trip as her "rite of passage" into adulthood. When I pointed out that she would be away from our family for five weeks, she simply said, "Oh. I thought it was for a year." This *did* take me by surprise. She was almost thirteen.

Amy believed that God was calling her as in Acts 1:8 "But you will receive power when the Holy Spirit comes on you; and you will be my witnesses in Jerusalem, and in all Judea and Samaria, and to the ends of the earth." She also quoted Matthew 28:19-20, "Therefore go and make disciples of all nations, baptizing them in the name of the Father and of the Son and of the Holy Spirit, and teaching them to obey everything I have commanded you. And surely I am with you always, to the very end of the age." She was solid in her spiritual walk, but she was so young to send with a bunch of strangers to another country. Thankfully, there was also the option of a one week mission trip. As parents, this was much easier to accept.

Since the cost was more than we could afford, Amy and I agreed to a "fleece." We prayed that if it was God's will for her to go, then He would somehow specifically provide for the airfare to Laredo, Texas without us first telling--or hinting--of the need to anyone but Him in our prayers. Two days later, we received a phone call from my brother-in-law. He told me that he had heard that Amy was hoping to go on an upcoming mission trip, and he wanted to offer a free airline ticket. How could he possibly have known? Amy had told her cousin, girl to girl, at a sleepover that she felt led to go on this trip. She said nothing about needing financial help or anything to do with airfare. Her cousin later happened to mention this conversation to her mom, who later told her dad. The dad called us, but we knew that the phone call was really straight from God. The registration was sent in!

Although this was not even a church mission trip, our own church sponsored her for half of the cost. Then, two days before Amy's necessary Typhoid shot, my sister handed me a collection of coins and bills their family had saved for "something special." They had no idea how much was in the container. We counted, and it totaled up to just over sixty-two dollars. The shot cost was sixty dollars, and we paid a dollar in tolls each way.

Another chunk of the trip cost was covered through a yard sale and by the donation of a couple's life-long penny savings. Still needing to raise the final amount, we received an unexpected phone call one day. The unsolicited total offered was exactly the amount we had left to pay. Amy's trip to Mexico was life-changing, and she experienced the blessing of leading three people to accept Christ.

In Awe of God

Cling to Christ for the Ride of Your Life!

There's No Way!

How can you step out in faith regarding missions?

Know His Way!

> ***Therefore go and make disciples of all nations, baptizing them in the name of the Father and of the Son and of the Holy Spirit, and teaching them to obey everything I have commanded you. And surely I am with you always, to the very end of the age.*** Matthew 28:19-20

> ***But you will receive power when the Holy Spirit comes on you; and you will be my witnesses in Jerusalem, and in all Judea and Samaria, and to the ends of the earth.*** Acts 1:8

> ***My help comes from the LORD, the Maker of heaven and earth.*** Psalm 121:2

In Awe of God

Write your own *KNOW HIS WAY!*

No Way!

Using the simple pattern below, briefly write your own story regarding missions. If your story is unfinished, leave those portions blank:

Before (There's no way!):

During (Know His way!):

After (No way!):

Extreme Home Makeover

Topics covered: *God's provision, body of believers, power of prayer, importance of testimonies, provision*

After moving into our dream house, my husband intended to put down tile flooring right away. His job loss shortly after we moved in began a financial roller coaster, which we rode for over nine years before finally recovering. Each time we approached the payoff of our revolving debt, another crisis hit, and we started all over again. With the addition of several hurricanes and tropical storms during that time, our house was in dire need of help.

The deductible for our homeowners' insurance was five thousand dollars in the case of a hurricane, and four hurricanes somehow weakened the exterior, but did no visible damage. When the following tropical storm hit, our kitchen was flooded as water poured through the west wall beneath the cabinets and linoleum. Conveniently, our deductible for a tropical storm turned out to be only five hundred dollars. The insurance completely paid to gut and repair our kitchen. Since Ron was able to do part of the work, and he paid a friend to do the rest, there was enough money left over to purchase the necessary tile for our whole house!

***

Once the kitchen and west wall were finished, Ron intended to conquer the tile installation during his vacation time that winter. As desperate as we all were for family vacation time together, this was his only window to work. We did not pray about this decision. I had seen how diligently Ron labored with great speed and agility to transform a room with tile, and I fully expected him to complete the project rather quickly. Somehow we would involve the family to make it fun.

At the tile store, we discovered they were closing for the week after Christmas, and we had no idea what to buy. With only an hour to decide and purchase flooring that would likely be in our house for the rest of its days, we somewhat panicked. Instead of accepting defeat, we hurriedly chose a large, dark tile with the thoughts that it would hide the dirt of eight pairs of feet traipsing all over it. Anxious to begin their vacation, the men loaded half of it onto Ron's pick up truck. He planned to unload it at the house and come back for the final batch. In the meantime, I stayed as the men loaded another pallet into the Suburban.

As Ron drove very carefully to the front of the parking lot out of our sight, the store owner fretted because the tailgate was not up. The tile was so heavy; surely it would not fall off. It was too late. As the truck turned onto the highway, almost the entire load dropped onto the road. With the help of a passer-by, Ron picked up the boxes of broken tile and shoved them back onto the truck. He returned to the store to tell us what had happened.

The store owner was beside himself with worry that we might demand our money back, but Ron assured the man that it was his own fault. With the tailgate back up on the truck and the Suburban loaded, the tile was brought to our house as planned. Ron would sort through what we had in order to salvage any whole pieces and box them together. We had six full boxes of broken pieces, but we now had another embarrassing problem. The tile looked terrible in the house. It was far too dark and the color matched nothing. Why hadn't we prayed and waited? Ron quickly called the store owner. After the holidays, we would return what we could, and then take our time to choose more carefully. We apologized again and wished him a Merry Christmas. What a relaxed, restful family vacation time we had at home, and the following week we found a beautiful light-colored river rock pattern that would be great at blending dirt.

***

While the tile had been purchased, we would have to wait for the next year's vacation to begin installation. During a heavy downpour one day, a large puddle appeared in the kitchen and another one in the middle of the carpet. The leaks in the wall had all been fixed. This could only mean one thing: water was seeping in from the foundation. With Ron's permission, I pulled up linoleum until I found the source of the leak. I immediately saw a large crack and signs of mildew spread across the entire kitchen floor. It continued to the carpet. Afraid to pull up anything else, I waited for Ron to come home from work before searching further.

The research ensued for how to repair foundation leaks. In the meantime, we scrubbed the ugly concrete floors with bleach and then invited our friends and neighbors to join us in signing it with permanent markers. What fun! It was soon covered with colorful pictures, our favorite Scriptures, as well as prayers for our home and all who would enter it. Little did we know at the time that it would remain that way for several months.

After completing his research, Ron did everything to prepare for his time off when he could again attempt to conquer the floors. Finally, the day arrived. Our neighbors pitched in to help us empty the house of furniture, and another friend donated the use of his ministry trailer to store it all. Ripping out the carpet revealed a much bigger project than we had imagined. Stemming from an outlet in the middle of the floor, four enormous cracks wove their way to the walls in each direction. In addition, across the back of the house, all along our two large sliding glass doors the foundation had crumbled away.

Next to Jesus, my husband is my hero. He is extremely intelligent and has been likened to a TV character, named MacGyver, who could make anything out of miscellaneous parts. Ron immediately borrowed the necessary tools from our generous neighbor, jack-hammered the crumbling concrete at the back doors, and perfectly replaced the edge of the foundation. He then began the set of steps to repair the floor crevices throughout the downstairs. This involved vacuuming, sweeping, and mopping—a lot of mopping! Lastly, a red "membrane" had to be painted inside the cracks and three feet on either side. It had to cure for a few hours. We then ran out of Ron's vacation days, and not one tile had been set.

Before he returned to work, there was an urgent problem needing a temporary fix. The red membrane could not be stepped on at all, or it would have to be redone, but its six foot wide painted rivers stretched all over the floor. Ron kindly set up make-shift balance beams across each one. From our bedrooms upstairs, one would have to step onto the first narrow bridge from the last stair. Other beams bridged the kitchen to the dining room to the living room to the bathroom and office. Another new adventure!

Because Ron could only work on this massive project in the evenings and on weekends, it took many weeks before the tile found its way to cover up those red masses. Until then, all eight of us perfected our balancing acts. I could run across three beams and the space in between them with a full laundry basket on my hip and a preschooler in my arms in order to get to the bathroom in time or to find the ringing phone. While others pitied us, we recognized the building of memories and the laughable stories we would never forget.

Nine months after the planned finish date, the tile was complete. During the monster project within the house, we began to receive notices from our Home Owners' Association about the need to replace dead grass patches and to paint the outside. The walls inside were also calling for paint. They were in line to be tackled next along with the baseboards. As we caught our breath before attempting to address anything else, Ron was sent on a business trip for three weeks. That is when our friends' plans unfolded quickly.

I was cautiously approached and informed that a group of our friends had prepared for a surprise attack on our house projects while Ron was away. Since my birthday fell during that time, they planned to tell my husband that it was a surprise for me, but we all knew that it was going to be a tremendous gift to him. Using donated paint left over from a community mission trip, I knew I would have to seek approval from my Home Owner's Association. We would have to work quickly to prepare for the scheduled workday. Amazed at the generosity of our friends, the HOA president did everything she could to deliver the approval in time. She and her husband even contributed to the project by paying the fee for the review.

I was told to prepare a detailed list of every project, both inside and outside the house. There were no guarantees, but the plan was to fill our home with volunteers and conquer as much as possible in one or two days before Ron's return. I purchased additional paint, a few plants, and other odds and ends, but everything else was donated. I was overwhelmed at the whole situation. My first "To do list" was returned to me, and I was told to add more to it—*everything* I could think of. That was awkward. I am much more comfortable on the other end of this sort of thing. I only fed everyone and ran any necessary errands. My brothers and sisters in Christ did the rest on that special Saturday.

Our neighbors watched in awe at the shocking sight as cars and people busily moved around like ants on a hill. Their curiosity was surely mixed with the appreciation that the house was going to look much better, too. They joined in. When all was said and done, seventeen adults, eleven teens, and five kids had all invested in our family beyond anything we could ever have imagined.

On the inside, every wall except the bedrooms and bathrooms had been painted beautifully, upstairs and down. On the outside, our two-story home had been pressure washed and perfectly cleaned, all cracks were sealed, and it was painted including the doors and all trim. The outside lamps were replaced and painted. All concrete was pressure washed, and the regular yard work was complete. In addition, a large portion of dead grass was replaced with new landscaping, mulch, and a place for stepping stones. Lastly, our family's neighborhood playground set was repaired, stained, and even given new swings, monkey bars, and gym rings. After many hours of preparation beforehand and twelve hours on Saturday, some returned yet again to complete the last few jobs in time.

As we returned from picking up Ron from the airport, it was dark outside, but our neighbors were out visiting in their driveways. Pulling up to the house, Ron immediately noticed the landscaping and looked confused. We then poured out the story. He choked up in awe at the enormity of this gift our family had received. We then gave him a tour of it all before he greeted some of the helpers who were watching his response. What relief flooded over my hard working husband!

***

Seven months later, Ron's parents and his sister came down from Georgia for my eldest daughter's high school graduation. For the first time since the flooded kitchen, we would have a party at our house. We were all so excited! As we bustled about days beforehand with the cleaning and food preparation that always precedes a house full of company, Ron feverishly worked to sand, paint, and install the baseboards on the entire main floor. We also took note of a few unfinished projects that were too much to tweak before the big day: Our mailbox was terribly rusty and in need of repair, the plants that had died in the winter freeze needed to be replaced, and the guest bathroom desperately needed paint and a way of hiding the ancient stained linoleum.

The next day after I had acknowledged the mailbox, my husband came home and asked me what had happened to it. Confused, we all went outside where our neighbors delivered the license plate number of a tow truck. Apparently it had swung around our cul-de-sac, completely knocking the mailbox off of the post, and the driver did not stop. The insurance paid us to fix it. Having noticed that the winter freeze had destroyed some of the young plants, Ron's dad replaced them and surprised us by filling in additional mulch and setting down a path of stepping stones. Inside, Ron's mom assisted with the baseboards and scrubbed and painted the guest bathroom. His parents even presented us with gorgeous new towels!

***

While some around the world live in huts of cardboard, and some have no home at all, we realize that to have a house is a blessing. A home that is safe and comfortable is wonderful, but above all, a place where loved ones meet together to laugh and to share each other's burdens is the greatest home on earth. I have had to ask myself repeatedly, "What is eternal about our house?" The answer is simple: "Those who enter it: God and the people." While we must work to maintain our home, the work to maintain our relationships has an everlasting affect, and all have beautiful results!

Extreme Home Makeover

Cling to Christ for the Ride of Your Life!

There's No Way!

What dissatisfactions with your home will you completely hand over to God?

How can you help another family with their home?

Know His Way!

> ***My Father's house has many rooms; if that were not so, would I have told you that I am going there to prepare a place for you? And if I go and prepare a place for you, I will come back and take you to be with me that you also may be where I am.*** John 14:2-3
>
> ***But as for me and my household, we will serve the LORD.*** Joshua 24:15b
>
> ***...there is a friend who sticks closer than a brother.*** Proverbs 18:24b

Extreme Home Makeover

Write your own *K**NO**W HIS **WAY!***

No Way!

Using the simple pattern below, briefly write your own story about your house or about the help of friends. If your story is unfinished, leave those portions blank:

Before (There's no way!):

During (Know His way!):

After (No way!):

The Baby Fix

Topics covered: *Provision, service, stewardship, and body of believers*

Just before summer, my high school graduate asked if she could apply for a job. The next day, without even applying, she was offered a part time job baby-sitting a toddler and an infant for the summer. The pay was exactly what she was hoping for. My other daughters filled in whenever needed, and all of us fell in love with these little ones. As the new school year approached, the girls would no longer be able to spend their days away from the house, and the mom searched for someone to replace them.

In keeping with our family tradition, each one of our kids was allowed to choose one extracurricular activity for the school year, in addition to our regular church functions. The four younger ones chose Upward Soccer, and the two older ones chose music lessons. We tallied up the total expenses and prayed for provision. With one in college now, our school budget was much tighter. My husband and I could not figure out a way for all six kids to do what they had requested. We would have to wait.

During my quiet time with the Lord one morning, I talked to Him about how much I enjoyed when the babies came to our house. I wondered if there was any way that we could blend them in with our family on a regular basis. There were definitely issues that would need to be resolved first. We already maxed out our Suburban; so, we could not fit in two extra car seats. How in the world could we still homeschool and keep the house quiet enough for my online college student? What if we tried and it didn't work out? I asked my mom to pray with me about it. I had not told my husband or kids what I was considering.

That same morning, when the mom dropped off her kids, she asked me if *I* would consider baby-sitting two days each week from afternoon to late evening at our house. I was shocked. She had always hired my daughters, not me. I told her that I had actually been praying about it, and then I shared my concerns. We agreed to a trial period. She told me the exact hours and pay, and she offered the use of one of her cars if we needed to go somewhere in an emergency. I told her I would pray about it.

I immediately called my mom to update that prayer request. While I calculated my expected earnings, my husband pulled up the extra expenses anticipated for the year. The numbers matched perfectly! Later that same day, my kids and I brought our little friends with us to the nursing home where we regularly visit. How did we fit in our vehicle? My husband had gone to work, and my oldest daughter was at home working on college class work. We fit just fine. Ron and I had both been praying about our decisions, and we presented the situation to our kids that night. It was unanimous. Everyone agreed to pitch in treating the babies as younger siblings and working as a whole family to earn the money for soccer, music lessons, and college.

After only the first week, we were all in love with our new routine. Rotating lessons and babies, we have all thoroughly enjoyed the gift of little ones regularly in our home once again. During their naptime, we do our group lessons, and when they are awake we all take turns tending to them. My little boy with five big sisters gets to feel like a big brother to a littler boy, showing him how to build train tracks and play cars and behave politely. We compete for the chance to bring giggles to their chubby little faces, and they have brought many smiles to ours. Twice each week now, our whole family is blessed with our baby fix. As an added bonus, we began soccer and music lessons, too.

The Baby Fix

Cling to Christ for the Ride of Your Life!

There's No Way!

What do you do when you must make a difficult decision?

Will you commit to lay your requests for wisdom before the Lord and wait expectantly?

Know His Way!

> ***The lot is cast into the lap, but its every decision is from the LORD.*** Proverbs 16:33
>
> ***In the morning, LORD, you hear my voice; in the morning I lay my requests before you and wait expectantly.*** Psalm 5:3
>
> ***Yet the LORD longs to be gracious to you; therefore he will rise up to show you compassion. For the LORD is a God of justice. Blessed are all who wait for him!*** Isaiah 30:18
>
> ***If any of you lacks wisdom, you should ask God, who gives generously to all without finding fault, and it will be given to you. But when you ask, you must believe and not doubt, because the one who doubts is like a wave of the sea, blown and tossed by the wind.*** James 1:5-6

The Baby Fix

Write your own *KNOW HIS WAY!*

No Way!

Using the simple pattern below, briefly write your own story about a decision in your life. If your story is unfinished, leave those portions blank:

Before (There's no way!):

During (Know His way!):

After (No way!):

Savor the Savior* and *KNOW HIS WAY!

Topics covered: *Ministry, dreams fulfilled, power of prayer, body of believers, God's perfect timing, neighbors, relationships, Christian teamwork, Great Commission*

I have dreamed of being an author since I was a little girl. I remember learning to write in my earliest school journal and pretending it was a "real" book. For an assignment in high school I wrote and illustrated my first children's story, and then another for a college class. While I never pursued publishing any of them, I always thought that "one day" I would follow that path. Because I absolutely love laughter, I mentally hung onto my own personal stories that tickled my funny bone. As my relationship with Christ grew, my experiences pointed so loudly to Him that I also tucked away those memories to add to my "one day when…" collection.

Although I am not a fan of solicitation, I also do not want to miss an opportunity to give as I feel led. Strongly focused on outreach through missions and serving, my church home encourages spiritual growth through solid Bible teaching. I truly love my church family; so, when the announcement was made that we were trying to raise the funds for a building to accommodate our blossoming congregation, I was not remotely offended. I was eager to somehow contribute—but how? We searched for any way to squeeze out some extra, but our options were minimal. Praying fervently for a way to help, one day it hit me clearly. I was so certain, that I filled out a commitment card with this promise: I would write the books that I had had in mind and send them out to publishers. All of the proceeds from the book that was first published would be a gift to my church building fund for life.

As I think about this offer now, it strikes me as laughable. Getting a first book published is a remote possibility. I knew how to write, but did not have a clue what to expect regarding the publishing process. I was taking a step of faith to even share what I was attempting. What if nothing ever got published? It was a chance that I would have to take, because I was absolutely sure that I was being called by God to obey in this way. Immediately, I began, but it was not the book I had always dreamed of writing. Instead, I felt compelled to prepare a manuscript about falling in love with Christ using a daily Bible study and journal method, which had changed my life.

As a busy wife and homeschool mom, I carried my book bag with me writing in bits and pieces everywhere I went. Thankfully I found a website where I could post my proposal for many Christian publishers to view at once for a six month time period for one set fee. Almost immediately I received a phone call with an offer, but there was a catch. Although recognized by the Evangelical Christian Publishers' Association, this was a smaller publisher specializing in new authors. Unlike larger publishing companies, they allow the authors to retain ownership of their work. Regardless of the fact that I would earn larger royalties with them, it would cost me two thousand dollars, which I did not have. I have learned through God's faithfulness, that where He guides, He always provides. I would wait and pray.

Three years after my initial conviction to write, our new church building had already been completed, and I had not yet contributed. During a focal week to update people on the building fund, I was deeply moved as our pastor spoke. I had been obedient. I had been sure of God's calling to write that book, yet it sat untouched in my book bag collecting dust. Within a period of eight days, four different people asked me what had happened with that book. Curious, I pulled it out for the first time in twenty months to see if it was even worth pursuing. It was.

The following Sunday morning, I cried out to God for wisdom. Suddenly a thought popped into my head. My heart beat loudly, and I dropped everything in order to follow through immediately. I typed a letter to our local Bruster's Real Ice Cream store owner asking if he would be willing to donate anything at all to support my new book. It had an ice cream theme. My family anxiously waited for me to print out the letter and seal the envelope, so I could deliver it on the way home from church. With the letter still in my bag, I was pulled aside after the service by someone who asked to remain anonymous. I was then given a sealed envelope with a card inside. The card explained that this person felt prompted by God to contribute to our church building fund by sponsoring my book. It contained a cashier's check for two thousand dollars! The following week, my book was in the hands of the publishing company and Bruster's had donated one hundred free waffle cone coupons!

***

Immediately after submitting my final manuscript for *Savor the Savior (Pen, Bible, Ice Cream!)*, I wondered what I should do next. I felt so strongly that this was not just about writing, but about speaking, teaching, and bottomless ideas for outreach. On a Sunday morning during my prayer time, I decided on the name of the ministry, *K**NO**W HIS **WAY**!*, which would be based on my third book. In my journal, I wrote a short, simple prayer asking if I should begin preparation right away with a website, or if I should wait and make it my New Year's resolution for 2011. I closed my prayers and went to church.

At a different service hour than usual, our pastor had laryngitis; so, the pastor of students preached. Based on Jonah, his sermon challenged us to start *now*, six weeks early, thinking about our *2011 Spiritual New Year's Resolutions*. He asked if we were willing to do our "big assignment that God was calling us to for the coming year," or if we were tempted to say, *"No way!"* Like Jonah, we could get it right the first time or the second time, but the risks would be the same either way; we may as well just *move forward now.* In addition, looking at what God had asked us to do in the past year we should evaluate what to do to adjust. *Wow!* I had gone to church at a different hour, listened to a different preacher, yet heard a message which spoke directly to me! *I set up the ministry website that same day.*

***

The week that my book, *Savor the Savior*, came out, my publisher proposed an idea. Knowing that I had been working on the other books, he asked me if I could complete the companion book, *Savor the Savior for Kids*, in order to present them both at the International Christian Retail Show. They would also match the covers of the first two books and advertise my third book—the one I had dreamed of writing. My publisher had generously compromised the cost in order to make this doable for us.

After much prayer and research ensuring this was all legitimate, we found that we could only pay our portion of the expenses by withdrawing from Ron's retirement fund. We had one week to decide. Recognizing that this was the open door to a dream coming true, I privately wept at the lack of provision. Desperate for prayer support, we feared that sharing the details would appear as a plea for donations; so, instead we sent out a very vague, but urgent prayer request.

Three days later, during a phone call, Ron was specifically asked for a book update. He explained that we were praying for clear direction regarding an offer, and the person prodded for further details. He was then put on hold. With the person's spouse calling out in agreement from the background, Ron was told to accept the offer--*they would cover the cost!* A special account had been set aside for "such a time as this."

***

As I approach completion of my dream book, *K**NO**W HIS* ***WAY!***, I realize that many of these stories had not yet happened when the idea came to me in the first place. God's perfect timing has supplied me with much more material as He has written my life story. I expect that there will be many more chapters, too!

Savor the Savior* and *KNOW HIS WAY!

Cling to Christ for the Ride of Your Life!

There's No Way!

What do you most feel called to do according to God's plan?

Know His Way!

You are my friends if you do what I command. I no longer call you servants, because a servant does not know his master's business. Instead, I have called you friends, for everything that I learned from my Father I have made known to you. You did not choose me, but I chose you and appointed you so that you might go and bear fruit—fruit that will last—and so that whatever you ask in my name the Father will give you. John 15:14-16

And we know that in all things God works for the good of those who love him, who have been called according to his purpose. Romans 8:28

As for God, his way is perfect: The LORD's word is flawless; he shields all who take refuge in him. Psalm 18:30

Savor the Savior* and *KNOW HIS WAY!

Write your own *KNOW HIS WAY!*

No Way!

Using the simple pattern below, briefly write your own story about your calling. If your story is unfinished, leave those portions blank:

Before (There's no way!):

During (Know His way!):

After (No way!):

AFTERWORD

The Happiest Ending Ever!

Topics covered: *Salvation, where will I go when I die, becoming a follower of Christ, and the Holy Spirit*

If you behave a certain way, does it mean that you will always have happy endings? No…and yes. Will you be happy if you get what you want, or if you get what God wants for you? Sometimes these are the same, but sometimes they are different. The only way to get everything you ask for is to only ask for one thing: God's will. If you trust that He knows best, you will find satisfaction with the results…eventually. If you are in the middle of one of your life chapters and the ending is not yet happy, then you can rest assured that the ending has not yet happened for that story. Some will not end at all until you pass into heaven, but how can you be sure to have *that* happy ending?

There's no way!

We are all in the same boat. Not one single person is perfectly free from sin, and since the payment for sin is death, we each desperately need to be rescued or saved.

> ***As it is written: "There is no one righteous, not even one***
> Romans 3:10

for all have sinned and fall short of the glory of God Romans 3:23

For the wages of sin is death, but the gift of God is eternal life in Christ Jesus our Lord. Romans 6:23

Know His Way!

Just as a drowning victim must cling to the life preserver, we must cling to our Life Saver, Jesus, believing He will rescue us.

If you declare with your mouth, "Jesus is Lord," and believe in your heart that God raised him from the dead, you will be saved. Romans 10:9

God made him who had no sin to be sin for us, so that in him we might become the righteousness of God. 2 Corinthians 5:21

For God so loved the world that he gave his one and only Son, that whoever believes in him shall not perish but have eternal life. John 3:16

No Way!

When a life is saved on earth, there is great celebration, and the person is fed and showered with gifts. But when a life is saved from hell and delivered to the kingdom of heaven, there is rejoicing like no other, the soul is spiritually fed and showered with heavenly gifts!

I tell you that in the same way there will be more rejoicing in heaven over one sinner who repents than over ninety-nine righteous persons who do not need to repent. Luke 15:7

If you then, though you are evil, know how to give good gifts to your children, how much more will your Father in heaven give the Holy Spirit to those who ask him! Luke 11:13

And hope does not put us to shame, because God's love has been poured out into our hearts through the Holy Spirit, who has been given to us. Romans 5:5

Cling to Christ for the Ride of Your Life!

So, what happens after we repent from our sins, say that "Jesus is Lord," believe in our heart that God raised him from the dead, and ask for His Holy Spirit to live in us? We will begin that roller coaster ride of our lives hanging on for dear life to Jesus. Along the way He transforms us bit by bit to make us more like Him. This process will not be complete until heaven--*The Happiest Ending Ever!*

The Happiest Ending Ever!

Cling to Christ for the Ride of Your Life!

There's No Way!

Are you certain of your own ending?

If you died today and were asked why you should be allowed into heaven, what would you say? *(Remember, it's not what you have done, it is the One you know.)*

Know His Way!

> ***Here I am! I stand at the door and knock. If anyone hears my voice and opens the door, I will come in and eat with that person, and they with me.*** Revelation 3:20
>
> ***Therefore, there is now no condemnation for those who are in Christ Jesus, because through Christ Jesus the law of the Spirit who gives life has set you free from the law of sin and death.*** Romans 8:1-2
>
> ***For God so loved the world that he gave his one and only Son, that whoever believes in him shall not perish but have eternal life.*** John 3:16

The Happiest Ending Ever!

Write your own *KNOW HIS WAY!*

No Way!
Using the simple pattern below, briefly write your happy ending story. If your story is unfinished, leave those portions blank:

Before (There's no way!):

During (Know His way!):

After (No way!):

APPENDIX

Tips for a Safe Ride

Topics covered: *Greatest commandment, Holy Spirit, baptism, church fellowship, Bible reading, God's peace, and bearing fruit*

According to Jesus, we are to obey His commandments, and these are the greatest:

> ***He answered, "'Love the Lord your God with all your heart and with all your soul and with all your strength and with all your mind'; and, 'Love your neighbor as yourself.'"***
> Luke 10:27

With His Holy Spirit living inside of us, we are to honor God.

> ***Do you not know that your bodies are temples of the Holy Spirit, who is in you, whom you have received from God? You are not your own; you were bought at a price. Therefore honor God with your bodies.*** 1 Corinthians 19-20

We are to be baptized as a picture of our new life in Christ.

> ***Therefore go and make disciples of all nations, baptizing them in the name of the Father and of the Son and of the Holy Spirit,*** Matthew 28:19

> ***Whoever believes and is baptized will be saved, but whoever does not believe will be condemned.*** Mark 16:16

We are to meet together regularly with other Christians.

And let us consider how we may spur one another on toward love and good deeds, not giving up meeting together, as some are in the habit of doing, but encouraging one another—and all the more as you see the Day approaching. Hebrews 10:24-25

We are to read and apply the Bible, God's Word.

But He answered and said, "It is written, 'Man shall not live on bread alone, but on every word that proceeds out of the mouth of God.'" Matthew 4:3-4

In Jesus, God's peace will guard our hearts and minds beyond our understanding.

And the peace of God, which transcends all understanding, will guard your hearts and your minds in Christ Jesus. Philippians 4:7

His Holy Spirit living inside of us will bear fruit, or show signs of His life within us.

But the fruit of the Spirit is love, joy, peace, forbearance, kindness, goodness, faithfulness, gentleness and self-control. Against such things there is no law. Galatians 5:22

Other Books by Jeri Daniel

TITLE: ***Savor the Savior***

ISBN: **978-1-59755-264-6**

PAGES: **84**

PRICE: **$10.00**

Do you spoon through gooey swirls in your favorite ice cream collecting clusters of candy?

Savor the Savior will teach you how to single out your favorite morsels from Scripture, savor each one, and praise the Lord, who lovingly prepared them. Many people struggle to keep a daily quiet time—not knowing where to begin or how to stick with it—but this enjoyable little book acts as your personal trainer, encouraging you enthusiastically as you go.

Stocked with samples, answers to common questions, and even a detailed leader's guide for four fun-filled group lessons, Savor the Savior is a handy and priceless resource. As you discover who God really is and how much He loves you, your relationship with Him will deepen.

Tap into an addictive means of meeting with the Lord on a personal level, and be prepared to develop an ever growing love for the One who truly loves you: Jesus Christ.

Order online at www.JeriDaniel.com

TITLE: ***Savor the Savior for Kids***

ISBN: **978-1-59755-270-7**

PAGES: **144**

PRICE: **$14.00**

Do you wish your kids would delight in the Lord as much as they delight in dessert?

Many people struggle to keep a daily quiet time – not knowing where to begin or how to stick with it - but as a companion book to *Savor the Savior*, this precious, little guide dishes up a variety of ways to develop lifelong habits for children of all ages.

Stocked with samples, answers to common questions, and even a detailed leader's guide for four fun-filled group lessons, *Savor the Savior for Kids* is a handy and priceless resource. As your kids discover who God really is and how much He loves them, their relationship with Him will blossom and grow deeper with time.

Introduce children to an addictive means of meeting with Jesus personally every day, and as they delight themselves in the Lord, He will give them the desires of their hearts.

Order online at www.JeriDaniel.com

Jeri Daniel is available for speaking engagements and personal appearances. For more information contact:

Jeri Daniel
C/O Advantage Books
PO Box 160847
Altamonte Springs, FL 32716

Jeri@knowhisway.org

Please visit the author's website at:
www.knowhisway.org

To purchase additional copies of this book or other books published by Advantage Books call our toll free order number at:

1-888-383-3110 (Book Orders Only)
or visit our bookstore website at:www.advbookstore.com

Longwood, Florida, USA
"we bring dreams to life"™
www.advbooks.com

www.ingramcontent.com/pod-product-compliance
Lightning Source LLC
Chambersburg PA
CBHW020857090426
42736CB00008B/406
* 9 7 8 1 5 9 7 5 5 2 7 1 4 *